ENGLAND

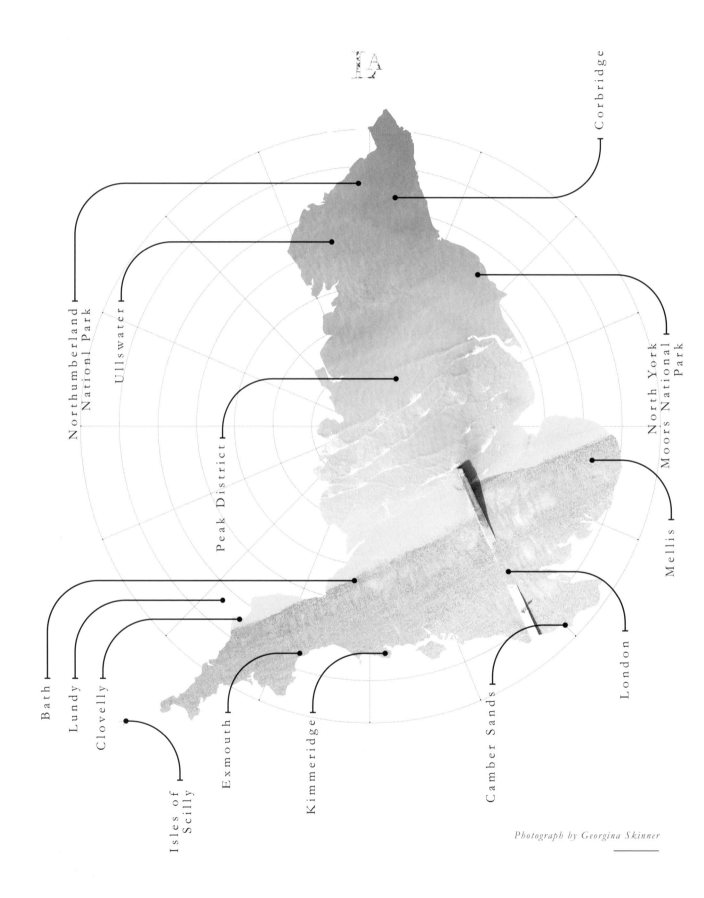

Corbridge

North York
Moors National
Park

Mellis

London

Camber Sands

Kimmeridge

Exmouth

Isles of
Scilly

Clovelly

Lundy

Bath

Peak District

Ullswater

Northumberland
National Park

Photograph by Georgina Skinner

EDITOR'S LETTER

Standing upon Bamburgh Dunes in windswept Northumberland, I watch three dogs bound over salt-softened grass to chase waves and gulls. In the distance stands Farne Island Lighthouse, a resolute silhouette before the late autumn sun. To my left are Holy Island's ruins, and to the right, there's nothing but boulders and sand. While there is a tea shop nearby, and a van selling cockles and whelks even closer, this isn't the 'pleasant pastures' or 'clouded hills' version of England I dreamt of when, all those years ago, back in Australia, I first considered the romance of distant shores. But it's one of the innumerable English scenes I now adore.

Although they've never been easy to pen, these editor's letters typically come to me - unexpected and rough - in a particular location. For France it was while ensconced in a Champagne châteaux, Japan happened when seeking solace along the Kumano Kodō, and for Scotland, it was when battling sleet upon the Isle of Skye. These settings all seemed, in those moments, to capture the soul of our chosen country. Yet England was different. This may be a tiny island but it's staggeringly diverse. It is sylvan, unpredictable, sublime, originative and contradictory - a land of eccentricity and ingenuity, a mix of worlds, practices and lifestyles all enriched and enlivened by an enthrallingly complex past. Travel here and discover more than you thought possible - and that defining *Englishness* is a daunting task indeed.

I mused on this opening while delving into Dorset's literary history, tramping across the Peak District and plotting journeys to distant islands. It could have been Cornwall's harbours, tales of Roman conquests, artistic movements born in seaside towns or star-filled skies that provided inspiration. But alone, in isolation, they never felt right, for England has many guises and no one scene, however iconic, quaint or quintessential it may be, entirely encapsulates this peculiar country. The land of hope and glory truly is the sum of its parts.

Which leads us back to a Northumberland beach. I'm writing this editor's letter here, in this moment, because I could have mulled over it indefinitely; trying to distil what makes England *England*, and determine what drove me to dedicate our very first issue, back in 2014, to this multifaceted, patchwork nation.

I have loved returning to that inaugural magazine, reimagining and revamping its content, matching contributors to the places they revere and the stories they've always wanted to tell. We've grown and evolved as a magazine - as things do and must - but still some features appear almost unchanged, like our pieces on Clovelly and Petersham Nurseries. Other destinations, such as the New Forest and Lake District, have been presented in an entirely new light. And then there are the stories that never made it into our original pages, for reasons I can no longer remember, that we have finally given space to.

Releasing this issue, having an excuse to once again explore my home, to ponder its whimsy and curious nature, may have been more challenging than expected. But it's been an honour. To be reminded how strange and exciting a place you thought to be 'definable' actually is, to reconnect with the immense talent that fills this island, to tell the tales of those equally devoted to English shores, to wander among sand dunes. That is reason enough to make a magazine.

- Liz Schaffer

COLOPHON

EDITORIAL & CREATIVE DIRECTOR
Liz Schaffer
liz@lodestarsanthology.co.uk

DESIGNER
Thomas Harrison

SUB-EDITORS
Sarah Kelleher, Miranda Keymer & Angela Terrell

CONTRIBUTORS
Tom Bland, Simon Bray, Tom Bunning, Piera Cirefice, Joel Clifton, Abi Dare, Sibel Ekemen, Robin Forster, Ana Gil, Orlando Gili, Graeme Green, Thomas Harrison, Jen Harrison Bunning, Isabelle Hopewell, Tanya Houghton, Lucy Howard-Taylor, Jim Johnston, Saara Karppinen, Sarah Kelleher, Cameron Lange, Jorge Luis Dieguez, Marina Marcolin, Annapurna Mellor, Joe Minihane, Claire Nelson, Diana Pappas, Annie Richards, Dan Richards, Owen Richards, Liz Schaffer, Liz Seabrook, Georgina Skinner, Renae Smith, Beth Squire, Angela Terrell, Kieren Toscan, Astrid Weguelin, Adam Woodward

COVER IMAGES
Tom Bunning

SPECIAL TYPE
Sibel Ekemen

DISTRIBUTION
Export Press
dir@exportpress.com

PRINT MANAGEMENT
Taylor Brothers, Bristol

PUBLISHED BY
This Is Magazine Limited

ADVERTISING & COLLABORATION
hello@lodestarsanthology.co.uk

 @lodestarstravel  @lodestarsanthology  /lodestarsanthology

ISBN: 978-1-5272-3139-9

www.lodestarsanthology.co.uk

CONTENTS

Photographs by Annapurna Mellor

FIRST IMPRESSIONS

Introduction by Liz Schaffer & Photographs by Beth Squire
Captions by Lucy Howard-Taylor, Betty Reid & Emile Woolf

This is a magazine about forests, crags and drystone walls; about culinary daring, crumbling ruins and journeys into the wild. It is an ode to literary histories and a smuggling past, coastal towns and cultural capitals. Recalling long forgotten giants and lingering lore, this is our homage to England and the verve that makes it eternal.

The words above were written for the inaugural issue of *Lodestars Anthology*; a short paragraph on our back cover designed to entice and intrigue, to hint at what might be found within the magazine's pages, then little more than a printed celebration of the land I was only just beginning to call home.

Lodestars began because I'd wanted to share England's splendour, explain what had drawn me here and reveal how the country shifted, seduced and fought definition, all the while remaining charmingly 'English' - comforting, familiar, a place with a past. The finished magazine also revelled in the wonders of travel and was created, in part, to remind readers that as dark and tumultuous as times may be, there is still beauty in this world; places, people and stories worth delighting in.

That said, *Lodestars* was never meant to last. Three issues were all I'd ever imagined producing. Yet returning to England, more than five years after summoning those first contributors, I am so glad it endured. The magazine has changed over time, but so has England, and as a result we can't recreate a perfect replica of Issue One - although we can share a few of the sentences that helped shape the *Lodestars* voice. I've paired these with photographs from Beth Squire, who joined the magazine in Issue Six. She grew up here and understands the fickleness of this country's lighting and moods - its ability to transform with the seasons. Her images depict an ancient land, all stone, weather and winding lanes. This is the England I moved across the world for, the one I always wanted to capture. Here's hoping our new issue enthrals and its old soul shines through.

To stand here during a winter sunset, while the surrounding fields glow and leafless trees create a dramatic natural frame, you can't help wondering if the fact that the Abbey has fallen into disrepair makes it all the more stunning. It is a testament to what was and what can never be completely destroyed. A place is as much about its spirit as stone, wood and long-gone treasures.

The scrambling terraces I had passed over on that first morning were the echo of John Davidson's, "With shelves for rooms the houses crowd,/Like draughty cupboards in a row", and my early morning nightingale was none other than John Keats' "light-winged Dryad of the trees". Coleridge taught me the difference between the lime tree and the ash, and John Clare worked me through wagtails and the virtues of the primrose. It is said that you can reach the soul of a place through its people: I found it through its poetry.

England is a place of firsts. The first snow or fallen leaf, the earliest daffodil and that blissful moment when you remember, after months of grey, just how wonderful sun on your skin can be. In this mighty green land the first day of a new season actually means something. It marks time, colours life and shapes the landscape in wonderfully photogenic ways. But the allure extends beyond those glorious beginnings.

It's the simple things that make this country great. Boiled egg and soldiers and lashings of Marmite are as English as Tube maps and tea cosies. No longer is our fair isle's gastronomic daring called into question, largely thanks to its ability to churn out foodie icons that taste as comforting as they look, are always in season and photograph remarkably well. Sometimes it is important to just take a moment and bask in the brilliance of baked goods and baked beans.

SAFE HARBOUR

Words by Angela Terrell & Photographs by Liz Seabrook

From the salt-caked seaside town of Clovelly springs creativity, beauty and a proclivity for adventure.

Sitting under the ancient beams in the snug bar of The Red Lion Hotel and listening to the jovial conversations echoing off the time-worn timber, you're transported to another era. An age when pirates and smugglers sat beneath these very eaves, telling swashbuckling tales of rum and jewels hidden along the pebbly coves of the rugged Devon coastline.

Clovelly would no doubt have been one of their mythical hideouts. Yet today, rather than a den of roustabouts and ne'er-do-wells, you'll find a friendly historic town branching off a sheer cobbled central street which runs up from a 14th century quay. Whitewashed cottages, most of which are heritage listed, have stood each side of this famous pedestrian street (also known as 'up along' or 'down along') for centuries. As you tread the ancient pebbles, many originating from the beach itself, you can so easily imagine the past and what may have occurred within the walls and alleys that surround you. Everything seems to lead to the sheltered harbour, which abounds in nets, buoys and cray pots. Boats come and go with both tourists and locals commanding brightly coloured timber fishing vessels named after lasses and legends.

Arriving on a summer evening gives you the opportunity to really discover the essence of Clovelly, free from the day-trippers who rightly flock here. Clematis dominates and foxgloves, daisies, wallflowers and irises burst from every window box. The picture-perfect shuttered cottages gleam in the gold of the setting sun, yet the early evening chill is enough to warrant the fires you can see glowing through the lace-lined windows. Sounds of laughter come from behind the front doors, as does the smell of freshly cooked seafood, which sends you back to The Red Lion for a feast of fresh crab sandwiches, thick with filling.

The Red Lion Hotel, which began its life as three cider houses, has suitably elegant accommodation. After a good night's sleep lulled by the sound of the sea, a crimson sunrise invites you to take an early morning stroll along one of the many walks that Clovelly has on offer. There is the choice of the Hobby Drive, which winds through lush woodland and provides magical vistas of the harbour, the Coastal Walk or the path to the majestic Clovelly Court Gardens, owned by the same family who for centuries have also owned the village.

Yet Clovelly is dedicated to tourism and is well set up to cater for the many people who come to bask in its beauty. A small entry charge helps maintain the village and includes entry to Clovelly Court Gardens and the two local museums. The Kingsley Museum must be explored; after all, this is the spiritual home of *The Water Babies*. If the cobbled road is too demanding for tired feet (cars aren't allowed in the village itself) there is a Land Rover service available, while donkeys take children up and down the steep cobbles in the summer months, and also help transport grocery shopping and slightly heavier supplies for those who call Clovelly home. Succumbing to the urge to visit this place - where natural beauty, whimsy and seafaring history merge so seamlessly - is wholeheartedly endorsed.

ENGLISH COUNTRY GARDEN

Words by Angela Terrell & Photographs by Georgina Skinner

Down by the river, a leisurely amble from Richmond, is a somewhat
unconventional garden centre.

Donning Wellingtons and wandering up narrow, stone-walled lanes feels decidedly earthy. And a little bizarre, as despite passing Thames-side water-meadows and seemingly forgotten royal estates, you're technically still in the confines of London. Yet these sometimes muddy lanes are worth the wading, leading you to a thoroughly English horticultural and gastronomic gem.

Petersham Nurseries is a haven of inspiration and a feast for the senses. Found by the grounds of Petersham House, you quickly become the proverbial kid in a candy store, wandering around and falling for the plethora of antiques, artworks, homewares and plants dotted around this Victorian working nursery.

Yet it's the culinary offerings that really lure visitors. Petersham Nurseries has two main foodie attractions - their award winning café and teahouse. The former, nestled inside a light-catching, bougainvillea-strewn greenhouse, is all about fusing naturally sourced organic produce with English cookery, slow food practices and Italian flavours. Many of the ingredients hail from Haye Farm in East Devon and are enhanced by edible herbs and flowers from the kitchen and cutting garden, with the menu itself paying homage to the seasons and often adjusted daily. Alternatively, the teahouse, which boasts a rather disarming dirt floor, is ideal for patrons hankering after something a little lighter.

It's not just the food that entices - the relaxed, stately setting is spectacular too. During my late summer visit the sight of freshly made peach Bellinis, sitting upon a marble-topped wrought iron table by the café's entrance, perfectly set the scene. The glass roof, with its ornate metal framework, suggestively reflected the colour and textures of the food below, and the eclectic mix of tables, chairs and antique collectibles filling the greenhouse made the café a setting to unwind in. Indeed, as I sat down to lunch the storm that had been looming unleashed itself, rain pattering rhythmically on the glass above as warm, exposed lightbulbs illuminated the space. The wild weather was fleeting but delicious, the cosiness palpable, the meal all the more sublime for the rain outside.

After a feast of Mozzarella di Bufala, with peaches, nasturtium and a dash of chilli, followed by wild turbot with heritage tomatoes, olives and agretti, and panna cotta made exquisite by basil and strawberries, I wandered through to the shop, besotted by its array of international wares. Girandole chandeliers hang from the ceiling and urns overflow with orchids and ferns. Vintage French mirrors open up the furniture-filled space, making use of the natural light that pours in on even the most overcast of days.

And then there's the nursery, where you can see how the earthy food you so recently indulged in came to be. There are seeds and herbs ripe for planting, so you too can make your own flavoursome creations, or at least grow something pretty. Dahlias, foxgloves and begonias mix with willowherb and cacti, each resplendent in the post-storm afternoon sun that sent low shadows over their playful sway.

Petersham Nurseries is an enchanting place where brilliant fare and the beauty of nature join to create a floral, food and art-filled experience to savour.

petershamnurseries.com

STONE & TIMBER

Words by Jen Harrison Bunning & Photographs by Tom Bunning

The allure of old spaces and grand designs.

Think of a self-catering holiday and where does your imagination take you? Perhaps it's to a shepherd's hut, pod or luxury yurt? All very appealing prospects, but if you're fortunate enough to be acquainted with the Landmark Trust, then your thoughts might head for more ancient dwellings. You may find yourself torn between a 19th century railway station in Staffordshire, a water tower in Norfolk or one of the few Jacobean houses in Spitalfields that survived the Great Fire of London. Maybe a converted pigsty in Yorkshire or a castle keep in the Devon estuary will take your fancy. Or you may settle on the great hall of a vanished manor house in a honey-stoned Somerset village.

The Landmark Trust is an architectural conservation charity with a simple mission: to rescue 'historic buildings that are at risk and give them a new and secure future.' Founded in 1965, in the midst of Beeching's decimation of the railways and the country-wide demolition of crumbling great houses, the Trust began when Sir John Smith, a young London MP with a passion for architecture, and his wife Christian, came up with what was, at the time, a fairly madcap plan. One to save buildings of domestic or industrial heritage that were too difficult, too remote, too small or not historically significant enough for the National Trust or the Ministry of Works to take on. The couple's aim was to preserve these properties, in their words, "not as museum pieces, to be peeked at over a rope, but as living places which people could inhabit as their own for short spells."

And that is what the Landmark Trust has been steadily doing for the last 50-odd years. From its first mission to save a Victorian cottage in Cardiganshire, there are now some 200 properties in the Landmark collection (mostly in the UK but with a handful on the continent), each sensitively restored to reflect its unique and fascinating past. It was one of their most challenging restoration projects that we were off to experience for ourselves; The Old Hall in Croscombe, deep in the heart of Somerset.

The village of Croscombe lies betwixt Wells and Shepton Mallet where the River Sheppey slices through the Mendip Hills. It looks wonderfully sleepy with its abundance of pretty stone cottages and houses dating back to Jacobean, Tudor and medieval times, their gardens teeming with scented jasmine, roses and wisteria.

The Old Hall can be found tucked away behind the church up a lane bound for the hills. Originally part of a baronial house built in around 1420, what remains stands in a tranquil walled garden with clambering roses, apple trees and a tumbledown graveyard. Once part of a fine home built for newly-weds, the vagaries of succession meant it passed between various wealthy families over several centuries, slowly falling into disrepair. A wing was lost, a chamber collapsed, but the Hall itself continued to be used as a meeting room for manorial business and later by a congregation of Baptists, who can be credited with first saving the building when they bought it in around 1730. Whilst they made permanent alterations to accommodate the chapel, they also took care of the property, re-plastering, painting and repairing the walls and ceiling. After the Second World War the congregation dwindled and the chapel passed into the hands of the church's District Association before being rescued by the Trust in the 70s and undergoing a huge restoration which involved unblocking doors, relaying floors, uncovering plasterwork, salvaging medieval windows and even covering over a baptismal well.

At the heart of the building is the hall itself, with its show-stopper of a Victorian roof. Creak open the door and your eyes are immediately drawn up to marvel at the five oak arched brace trusses vaulting overhead. Covered by a false ceiling for hundreds of years, the oak has never been stained and its natural rich tones combine with ochre-tinted rough plaster walls, a red quarry tiled floor and late summer light streaming in through giant windows to give a wonderfully warm and welcoming effect.

At the east end of the hall, you step through to what has, in its various incarnations, been a buttery, vestry and perhaps once a stable and school house too. It is now a simple but well-equipped kitchen with a pale grey flagstone floor and handsome furniture. At its centre is a hearth with an ancient, blackened stove that no longer fires but looks most pleasing - and there's a modern galley with all the essentials tucked around it.

Up the winding staircase are two modest bedrooms, a deliciously dark double tucked at the back and a triple with a sweet shuttered window and views of the church to the front, both with original fireplaces, hand-printed curtains and charming lamps converted from old stoneware.

Despite the historic nature of the Hall and its delicate restoration, its spaces are designed for living in and, whilst the furnishings are attractive and of high quality, nothing here is too good for daily use. This is interior design that will never go out of style, all fashioned to complement the glorious old bones of the building. And this home-from-home appeal is no accident. As Landmark's Furnishing Manager John Evetts wrote for an issue of *Listed Heritage* magazine, "I hope that visitors bring something of their own to the buildings for the few days in which they inhabit [them] . . . so I like to leave empty spaces in which they can position them." Pegs

await shopping bags, garments and dog leads, jugs await flowers and racks await boots.

It's true that The Old Hall lacks what some might consider to be modern-day essentials: there's no WiFi or television and little reception, but most fun and relaxation usually happens when you cut yourself off from technology for a short while and appreciate what's right in front of you. If you were desperate you could easily walk up the hill or down to the pub to get a signal, but why would you? (Unless it's just an excuse to have a top-notch basket of scampi at The George Inn.)

On our last evening, carrying cameras, notebooks and a bottle of rosé, we tramped up the hill to toast the end of a dreamy long weekend. Settling on a ridge overlooking the village, we watched the day fade into silvery dusk and agreed that this was England at her most seductive - wondering, not for the first time, just why we were heading back to London in the morning.

Given the enormous range of self-catering properties available, why choose a Landmark? Well, there's not enough space within these pages for a full rhapsody, but you're unlikely to find such a range of

quirky and interesting places to stay on offer anywhere else. And every stay makes a difference to the Trust, so you'll have an added feel-good glow from knowing you're helping to rescue historical buildings for future generations.

Go with family or friends to a castle or manor house and spend a week feasting at long tables, stomping about in the mud and playing furious games of Scrabble. Go and explore a town or city with a weaver's cottage or parsonage as your base. Go *à deux* to a bolthole for a romantic weekend or, given how reasonable the rates are, venture alone to a medieval chapel for a dose of solitude.

John and Christian's original aim was to rescue what they called "unfashionable" properties, but as we gallop through the 21st century with all of its bells and whistles and throwaway consumables, the sort of pared-back, comfortable stay you'll experience at a Landmark has unwittingly become on trend. At least to those of us who seek simplicity, appreciate well-made things, and take pleasure in the unchanging nature and quiet beauty of ancient buildings and their surroundings.

landmarktrust.org.uk

THE ISLES

Words by Kieren Toscan & Photographs by Renae Smith

Made up of well over 100 islands, and with a history rich in daring and drama, the Isles of Scilly feel like a world forgotten.

Such tales conjured visions of rough seas and dense fog, yet supposedly it was also a destination with pockets of the same soft quaintness that defines the English countryside.

The hollow whirr of the aircraft's propellers filled the cabin, the sound first bouncing off the buildings around us before settling to a dull roar as we reached the start of the runway. A controlled push of the throttle by the pilots sent us on our way, up and over the green ocean with its serpent-like scales of waves and white peaks, and onwards towards the Isles of Scilly.

Renae and I had heard stories of these Isles from fellow travellers over the years - a setting that seemed sacred, far-flung, shrouded in lore and ingenuity. Around 50 kilometres southwest of the mainland, we were told that this was a rugged, weather-beaten place where some 500 ships, likely many more, had been wrecked over the centuries. Such tales conjured visions of rough seas and dense fog, yet supposedly it was also a destination with pockets of the same soft quaintness that defines the English countryside. We had been assured that some of Scilly's white sand beaches could rival the best of the tropics, although you couldn't enjoy the azure waters as it was always too cold to swim. So we didn't quite know what to expect upon landing but hoped for something special.

The flight to St Mary's gave us an excellent introduction to the archipelago. From our high vantage point we could see the other inhabited islands - Tresco, St Martin's and Bryher to the northwest, and St Agnes further south. Littering their surrounds were some 140-odd islets and rocky outcrops, spelling danger to unsuspecting sailors but providing safe havens for birds and colonies of seals.

We had assumed that things would be quiet when we arrived - after all, the Isles' population numbers just over 2,000 and the tourist season had not yet begun in earnest - but found its principal settlement, Hugh Town, to be a hive of activity. We suspected this was partly due to the excellent weather but mostly because preparations were being made for the annual World Pilot Gig Championships the following week. Gigs - colourful, six-oared rowing boats used in the past to take pilots out to incoming ships, which they would then help navigate to shore - would soon be raced between the islands and the population would swell, if only for a few days.

From the harbour we watched some of the crews make their way south as they trained, straining against the waves as they rowed in unison. We followed their lead and took the ferry, also south, to St Agnes and its neighbouring Gugh, which are joined by a sandbar at low tide. With stunning views back to St Mary's the landscape here changed quickly, moving from marine heath to lush farmland as we journeyed along the island's central country lanes, all of which seem to lead to Troytown Farm, the

UK's southernmost settlement and, therefore (and some would say most importantly), its southernmost ice-cream maker. Soon after making this discovery, we were sitting in the balmy afternoon sun greedily devouring our spoils whilst gazing over the rocky islets and further out to sea.

With tides and ferries being the arbiters of one's travels between the Isles, it wasn't until early afternoon the following day that we arrived on Bryher, which only measures half a mile at its widest point. Having checked in at the Hell Bay Hotel, a contemporary, welcoming abode adorned with artworks from the Newlyn and St Ives schools of art, we charted a course along the island from head to toe. We made our way over Bryher's burnt-tip of low olive scrub, and then south through a compact countryside of farmlets, wildflowers and ferns; treading carefully around nettles - with success - and honesty boxes selling local fudge - with much less. As we neared the hotel, we stopped along a beach to test whether it was indeed too cold to swim. The water proved surprisingly bearable and we spent the evening debating, over a scrumptious meal and one too many wines (the Hell Bay Hotel has three AA rosettes), if dipping a single toe into the Atlantic that afternoon was enough to truly gauge the temperature, but found willing volunteers for a more substantial test hard to come by.

As if it was choosing sides, the sun retreated the very next day and clouds slowly built to take its place. The temperature dropped, the sea grew grey and a storm announced its impending arrival with winds that continued to strengthen as we reached Tresco. Yet with so much still to see we pushed on, reaching Tresco Abbey Garden just as the rain started. Sheltered by towering trees and surrounded by 20,000 plants

from across the world's sub-tropical climate zones, the hours slipped away as we meandered along the paths, lost in thought and the beauty that surrounded us.

Outside the protection of the garden, we found that the weather had worsened considerably. Leaning into a gale that lashed us with rain, we headed north, with Cromwell's Castle in our sights, but soon realised the futility of our plight - this was not sightseeing weather. Seeking shelter at The New Inn, Tresco's only pub, we settled in for the night, bottle of red wine in hand, while the rain flicked the windows and the wind howled.

However, as quickly as it had arrived, the wild weather dissipated and we awoke the following morning to bright sunshine, which presented the perfect opportunity for a day trip to St Martin's. Against a backdrop of crystal clear cyan water, we walked its pristine white beaches, the fine sand soft and warm against our bare feet. A stroll back along the island's spine soon found us once again amongst farmlets and their pocket square-sized, hedgerow-adorned fields, remnants of the flower trade from years gone by, providing a strange contrast between rural and the quasi-tropical barely a stone's throw away.

Too soon, it seemed, it was time to journey home to the mainland. Yet just before our departure, the fog crept in, eerie and mythic, casting doubt as to whether we would make it back for our ferry or be stranded for another day. It cleared just in time but, given our first taste of the Scillies, wouldn't it have been joyous if it had decided to stay?

hellbay.co.uk
tresco.co.uk
visitislesofscilly.com

"

Leaning into a gale that lashed us with rain, we headed north, with Cromwell's Castle in our sights, but soon realised the futility of our plight - this was not sightseeing weather.

"

A RIVER RUNS THROUGH IT

Words by Claire Nelson

Illustrations by Astrid Weguelin

Seeking the source of the Thames.

All rivers have to start somewhere. This occurred to me one cool London afternoon, leaning on the wall beside Tower Bridge as it raised its arms to let a tall ship pass through. I was familiar with the Thames River and its beeline for the sea but realised, in that moment, that I didn't actually know where this waterway began.

So I decided to find out - which, it turns out, is easy enough to do. There is a dedicated National Trail, the Thames Path, that follows the course of the river, all 184 miles of it. It takes two weeks to walk the entire thing but for me it became a project to dip in and out of, walking it in segments over a year or so, travelling from station to station and through all seasons.

It was summer when I set off, heading west through London, past the gilded spires of Westminster, picking my way through the merry throngs outside Richmond's riverside pubs and around the leafy border of Kew Gardens. Shortly I passed Eel Pie Island, the bohemian home of a small population of artists as well as the setting for both Rolling Stones gigs and Charles Dickens's *Nicholas Nickleby*. Once past Teddington's weir and footbridge, the Thames ceases to be tidal; it simply, in the English way, keeps calm and carries on. A supermarket trolley half-submerged in the water welcomed the urban section through Staines, a concrete wonderland of shops and traffic, the Thames slipping past largely unnoticed.

I returned to the trail in autumn, from Windsor, the castle silhouetted against a hazy sky. The name Windsor comes from the Anglo Saxon for 'winding shore', a tribute to the twisting, turning river. Here it was high, swollen along its banks. I suppose this must have once been a top place for swimming, as I spotted an old, weather-worn Etonian sign: 'Boys who are undressed must either get into the water or behind screens when boats containing ladies come in sight'.

In Berkshire I passed Boulter's Lock; at 200 metres it is the longest lock on the Thames. A little further along, the path veers away from the river into Cookham, where Kenneth Grahame lived while writing *The Wind in the Willows* - Toad Hall was inspired by the nearby Lullebrook Manor, whose owner famously possessed what was then the only motor car in the village. The evening was spent bunked down in a local B&B run by a retired crime novelist and his wife, where a cup of tea revived the senses and socks and shoes dried beside the radiator.

The weather hadn't let up the following day. From Marlow, flooding had drowned the path completely and there was little option but to wade through it, mocked by the presence of swans gliding by unperturbed. The river had swelled so far beyond its borders that it was impossible to differentiate between riverbank and field. But once socks and shoes are wet one might as well plough on and by the time the river came to my knees I was resigned to being soaked - and much like the swans I rather enjoyed myself.

I picked the May Bank Holiday weekend to walk from Reading, a town which has hosted Jane Austen and Oscar Wilde, in a boarding school and prison respectively. The Thames Path took me into Pangbourne, where Kenneth Grahame lived out his final years -

> *Once past Teddington's weir and footbridge, the Thames ceases to be tidal; it simply, in the English way, keeps calm and carries on.*

for his funeral, the local church was decorated with willows collected from the edge of the Thames. Today the sunshine had drawn people to the water and in Goring-on-Thames the wide river was busy with narrowboats and bordered by cafes bursting with weekenders brunching under the shade of patio umbrellas. The path wound through meadows, sometimes veering away from the river for a while but always returning. I camped overnight in Wallingford and woke in the morning to torrential rain. I sloshed past the roaring white water of Benson Lock's mighty weir, followed by the crumbling remains of Wallingford Castle - sister to Windsor and the site of much Royal infighting, it was destroyed in a four month siege in 1652. There is no sign of drama here now. Unless you count the weather.

———————

Winter was in full swing when I braved a day's walking from Shillingford; the air was crisp, the landscape pale and frosty. Once again the river had flooded its banks, drowning fields, sheets of ice shimmering in the early morning sunshine. A horse stamped on an ice-bound pond, shattering it to take a drink. It was too cold for wading but thankfully a raised wooden walkway had been installed to rescue Thames Path ramblers. Shillingford's Grade II listed stone bridge looked a picture surrounded by fields of frost while, further down the trail, the thatched-roofs of Dorchester village made the whole place seem frozen in time.

———————

Conditions were better once I tackled the Oxfordshire section. It was early summer and the Thames Path weaved through bucolic scenes - fuzzy grey cygnets trailing mother swans and lush green fields heavy with seeding dandelions. After a while I reached Godstow Abbey, built in 1133 and eventually ruined in the English Civil War. In its heyday it was the home of Rosamund Clifford, King Henry II's beautiful mistress, who died here

at only 30 years old (legend has it the Queen poisoned her, though that's most likely folklore scandal).

Newbridge, despite its name, boasts the second oldest bridge on the river and waymarks the vine-draped Rose Revived pub, which flaunts an expansive riverside beer garden that was too inviting to resist on such a warm afternoon. That night I camped at Shifford Lock, by prearrangement with the lock-keeper, and the morning arrived bright and beautiful. The trail ventured through grassy, wooded countryside to the chocolate box village of Kelmscott where Arts and Crafts artist William Morris lived for the last 25 years of his life, collecting reeds and plants along the riverbanks to use in his pattern work.

———————

It was autumn when my boots hit the path for the final stretch. This was Gloucestershire, and the Thames was now a muddy stream, no more than five metres wide and interrupted with patchy islands of grass. At St John's Lock, near Lechlade, I was met by a statue of a reclining Father Thames, a bearded, god-like figure harking back to the bygone age of river worship. As I carried on, the river became smaller and smaller, until it was nothing more than a trickling stream passing the overgrown gardens of rural residences.

In a quiet, grassy field at Trewsbury Mead stands a gnarled old ash tree, one branch reaching toward a weathered stone, marking the source of the Thames. When I reached it, the ground was dry. The infant Thames was somewhere just below the surface, mere groundwater, working its way quietly towards London, growing in stature and strength until mighty enough to carry tall ships to sea. I like the idea that even in the smallest, quietest things there is potential for greatness. It's good to remember we've all got to start somewhere.

> *Once again the river had flooded its banks, drowning fields, sheets of ice shimmering in the early morning sunshine.*

A MIDSUMMER NIGHT

Words by Diana Pappas
Photographs by Diana Pappas & Tom Bland

The thrill of returning home.

I am standing in the centre of an old hay meadow, surrounded by buttercups, clover and English plantain as the sun dissolves into the misted horizon. The gradual handover from day to night has begun. Countless rabbits watch me, warily, darting in and out of their burrows, and yet the swallows seem untroubled by my presence, patrolling the skies for insects. Trees at the forest's edge look on, unmoving, but the grasses shiver. I too can feel the cool easterly breeze on the back of my neck. A moth floats past in search of a favoured wildflower and I settle in to watch this June evening unfold. There are the faint sounds of agriculture, farmers taking advantage of the dry weather and long daylight hours to cut, turn and bale hay, preserving summer at its peak for the wild and wintery days ahead. As the blackbirds, wood pigeons and sheep bid each other goodnight, the colour drains from the distant hills, a myriad of greens turning various shades of graphite. Wisps of peach clouds become a dusty rose, then a glowing salmon pink, before surrendering to the half-light. A curlew flies overhead, making its way back to its nest on the moor, and I too decide to head home.

When we come to Northumberland in England's northeast, it's always for a month, and this time we're here in the weeks leading up to midsummer. Northumberland is expansive and varied, with Roman ruins, castles and a dramatic coastline, and on previous trips we wouldn't hesitate to set off into the unknown, hungry for adventure.

But we have a baby now and it's a different trip this time. We take one camera instead of two and spontaneity gives way to thoughtful consideration of nap times. Trips further afield seem a bridge too far, so we content ourselves with our little corner of Northumberland, claiming a spare room in Tom's childhood home, just north of the County Durham border.

Staying local means exploring the familiar and for the first time I take full stock of the many ecosystems just beyond the garden, a stone's throw from the stone house, over the stone walls. There is the old hay meadow but also forest, fell, moor, heath, pasture, bog and woodland; the ever-changing patchwork quilt of the natural world, stitched together by hedgerows and drystone walls, old roads, byways and public footpaths. All it takes is an engagement of the senses to look, listen, smell, touch and sometimes taste what nature has to offer.

Tom's family has untold names for the walks they take from their front door. There's the forest track, the mushroom walk, the green lane. We can loop around the field or along the gorse path, up the hill, over the moor. Each time we return to the house we recount what we have encountered - a bullfinch, a hovering kestrel, two hares darting out of sight, a cep mushroom. Sometimes the nature sightings are so extraordinary that the walk has to be repeated the next day, and the day after that, everyone looking out for the barn owl at the bottom of the field that Tom

" There are also subtle disappearances - the fading bluebells, the "
fallen apple blossoms, the last call of a cuckoo before it flies
south to Africa, almost leaving without us noticing.

saw the previous night. But it eludes us, constantly. We bring back leaves and seed pods to look up in naturalist books and spend days wondering if we have identified an English or a wych elm. We stop to smell sweet cicely or take a bite of lemony wood sorrel, carefully avoiding brushing against the stinging nettles - but, of course, we adore the Northumbrian nettle cheese they enhance. We resolve to make elderflower wine, or at least elderflower vinegar, and eye ripening currants, gooseberries and strawberries with anticipation. The south of England will already be gorging on these fruits but up north we must be patient.

Each day there is an exciting new reveal - the first foxglove in flower, the first red admiral butterfly, the first chirring of a nightjar. There are also subtle disappearances - the fading bluebells, the fallen apple blossoms, the last call of a cuckoo before it flies south to Africa, almost leaving without us noticing.

Some creatures we hear and seldom see, like the nightjars, and others we see and rarely hear, like a barking roe deer. Then there are the truly mysterious, the red squirrels and tawny owlets. We get brief glimpses of skylarks as they ascend out of sight into the bright blue above, singing, trilling and toasting the English summer. At night we listen to the chatter of birds in the poplars just beyond the house, unless the wind has kicked up and then the only conversations we can hear are those of the trees in and around the forest.

Willow, aspen, alder, silver birch, Scots pine, larch and oak, rowan, hawthorn, elm and ash; the trees around us are displaying every shade of green, full of new leaves, needles, seed pods and pinecones. Beneath the canopy are unfurling ferns, budding heather, tough brambles and carpets of moss. The verges are full of flowering umbels of wild carrot, cow parsley and cow parsnip, indistinguishable to the untrained eye. The gorse is a sea of yellow blooms, filling the air with its heady, coconut scent. Summer here is lush and verdant, vibrant and varying.

It has been a perfect June and it is with some reluctance that we pack our suitcases to head back home across the Atlantic. We savour the last few long days of midsummer, squeezing in a walk whenever we can. We have had so much sunshine that cloud or mist is a welcome change, reason enough to venture out once more.

Late on our last night, after our daughter is fast asleep, we look out of the window and see mist filling up the Tyne Valley. It engulfs hillside after hillside as it climbs steadily up the fields towards the house. Looking isn't enough, I need to be immersed in it, so I set out along the track, down the hill and into the lower field. The waist-high grasses are wet and windblown and each step forward soaks my clothes a little more. Suddenly a lavender light breaks through and the mist lifts just enough to reveal a corner of the field. There, perched on a fence post, is a barn owl, the barn owl we have been searching for, glowing white against the dusky palette. For a minute or two I go unnoticed and drink in the atmospheric sighting, but my excitement gives way to the stinging realisation that our trip is coming to a close and this gorgeous English summer will continue on without us. The barn owl takes off and silently makes its way along the line of oaks at the forest's edge, weaving between them before disappearing into the night.

THE EDGE OF ENGLISHNESS

Introduction by Lucy Howard-Taylor & Photographs by Jorge Luis Dieguez

Everyone has a childhood memory of being by the sea, spade in one hand, ice-cream dribbling in the other. Nostalgia is as essential to the seaside as the golden fug of fish and chips on the breeze, or grazing one's feet on winkles. And yet, for an experience so shaped by tradition, going to the beach for relaxation and pleasure is a relatively modern phenomenon. We have for most of our history feared the edge of solid ground and, as the gateway to the perils of the ocean, the shore remained unknowably wild. It was only in the late 18th century that this attitude started to shift, as the perceived medicinal value of sea air and water saw them prescribed for conditions as varied as depression and gout. Over subsequent decades, the rise of the railway also made it possible for more people to travel.

It was the Victorians who 'made' the seaside, fashioning grand pavilions, piers and promenades to cater for increasing numbers of merry holiday-seekers from further and further afield, who took dedicated city-to-shore express trains (the 'Sunny South Express' ran from Liverpool to Brighton, the 'Kentish Belle' from London to Ramsgate) in search of fresher air and languid days far from the urban scrum.

The seaside holiday beloved of generations was born here, in England. And while it broadly follows the same pattern wherever you are (sit in the sun, dig in the sand, swim in the sea), in this country alone it retains some of its strange, native magic. The bathing machines may have been converted into pastel-painted beach huts and the Punch and Judy shows are fewer and further between, but you can still ride a donkey along the sand on Weymouth Beach and break your teeth on gluey 'seaside rock' in Brighton.

Even after decades of declining tourist numbers born of the boom in affordable international air travel, the coast remains a quintessential expression of Englishness in all its charm, eccentricity and affable tolerance of discomfort - come wind, rain or shingled shore. And of all England's coastline, perhaps none is more beautiful and varied than that of the south. From the wide, hairy dunes of Camber Sands, to Dorset's tumbled coves and the limestone bluffs of Beachy Head, this is the iconic English seaside at its best. The water may be cold, the weather unpredictable, and the pre-fab snack huts reliably quaint, but the simple, ballooning joy of a sunny day spent with the ones you love within breath of the sea will never not be wonderful. Here, everyday routines are put aside and the seaside feels less like the physical reality of land ending and water beginning as it does a condition, a way of being in the world that is as free and encompassing as the tide.

INDUSTRIAL GIANTS

Words by Abi Dare & Photographs by Owen Richards

An area of rugged, natural splendour and a walker's paradise, the Peak District's tale involves more than spa towns, tramping and vistas.

Stretching across a large swathe of Derbyshire and poking into parts of Cheshire, Staffordshire and South Yorkshire, the Peak District formed Britain's first national park upon its creation in 1951. It encompasses two very different faces. To the north lie the imposing gritstone ridges and brooding moorland of the Dark Peak, to the south are the softer limestone tors, wooded dales and emerald-green pastures of the White Peak. Both are breathtakingly beautiful, but hidden amongst their soaring slopes, craggy cliffs and picturesque villages are the remnants of industries that helped shape history far beyond this corner of England. For this is no pristine wilderness but a landscape that has been lived in and worked on for millennia.

Growing up in the Peak District, I was fascinated by the ghosts of this industrial past. Indeed, they defined my world as a child. The trail where my brothers and I used to ride our bikes was the former Cromford and High Peak Railway, once used to transport minerals. The strange walls in the woods behind our house, which our imaginations transformed into castles and forts, formed the shell of an old engine house. Even our school was a legacy of industry, having been built in the 18th century for millworker children, and our daily walk to lessons took us past gushing drainage soughs and neat rows of weavers' cottages.

The presence of heavy industry in such a rural area is hardly surprising when you look at the ring of metropolises - Manchester, Sheffield, Birmingham, Derby, Nottingham - that encircle the park. In fact, it was at the southern tip of the Peaks, in the Derwent Valley (now a UNESCO World Heritage Site), that the Industrial Revolution sprang to life in 1771, when Sir Richard Arkwright opened the world's first water-powered cotton mill in the village of Cromford. But the region's industrial heritage stretches back much further than this.

Quarries are thought to have been in operation in the Peak District since the prehistoric era, producing gritstone for buildings, millstones (once used to grind grains and now the symbol of the national park) and, more recently, aggregate for roads and motorways. The limestone hills of the White Peak are also rich in lead ore, which has been mined since Roman times - first by numerous small-scale shafts dug by individual families (local custom enabled miners to excavate anywhere, except underneath gardens, orchards, highways and churchyards), and later by larger mines powered by steam pumps and gunpowder. Roman ingots originating from the Peak District have been discovered as far afield as Normandy, and a significant proportion of the lead used for the medieval boom in cathedral construction was sourced from the area.

And then came the textile trade. With its surging rivers and deep gorges, the Peak District was the ideal location for the early water-powered mills - and the miners' wives and children provided a ready pool of labour. Yet as technology advanced, the narrow valleys proved unsuitable for larger steam mills, leaving the region untouched by the rapid urbanisation which transformed once-sleepy towns such as Manchester into smoke-belching cities. Regardless, small-scale weaving and spinning continued into the 1900s.

Apart from several active quarries, whose operations have become increasingly contentious in recent years, most of these industries have long since vanished. But traces of them are still clearly visible in the landscape - in the canals and disused railway lines that criss-cross the countryside, in the grassed-over hollows and hillocks, and in the pick-marked tunnels, now playgrounds for cavers and potholers, which lace the rocks. These scars don't detract from the beauty of the park. Rather, they form an inherent part of it, and many are now vital habitats for flora and fauna. Beneath ground, old mines provide roosts for bats, above, wildflowers and rare lichens thrive on the mineral-rich soil of former waste heaps.

For me, nowhere is more symbolic of this co-existence between nature and industry than Lathkill Dale, where my parents and I used to forage for sloes. Here, the crystal-clear River Lathkill springs out of a cave and burbles its way along a wooded valley flanked by high limestone ridges where ravens nest. The first things to catch your eye as you wander are moss-covered waterfalls and a series of weirs and pools created to trap fish, but look closer and you'll spot unusual dips and walls between the trees - all that is left of the mines, processing plants and engine houses that once made this tranquil spot a hive of noise and activity. And that's not all. Standing on the opposite bank to the footpath are the eerie ruins of Bateman's House, the home of a 19th century mine agent that straddles a former shaft. A little way further on, crumbling stone pillars mark the course of an aqueduct which once powered the giant wheel of Mandale Mine.

If you want to get even closer to the region's industrial past there are several fascinating museums to visit. The Peak District Mining Museum in the village of Matlock Bath has replica tunnels which you can crawl through to glimpse the harsh, claustrophobic life of a miner. Just down the road, Masson and Cromford Mills are now visitors' centres with working machinery whose rhythmic clacking echoes off the bare walls. And outside the town of Wirksworth lies the National Stone Centre, which sits in a former quarry dotted with fossils and geological formations.

So, if you head to the Peak District, take the time to appreciate not only the beauty of the landscape but the industries and human stories whose impact extended far and wide. Think of the miners who toiled away in the damp and dark, of the mill owners whose vision transformed Britain, and of the thousands of millworkers who laboured under gruelling conditions to make it a reality. Their names may have been largely forgotten but their legacy lives on.

> "
> *Beneath ground, old mines provide roosts for bats, above, wildflowers and rare lichens thrive on the mineral-rich soil of former waste heaps.*
> "

PLAYTIME

Introduction by Cameron Lange & Photographs by Orlando Gili

In August 1976, even before The Rolling Stones played their famous 30-song set at a scorched Knebworth Fair, the two-hundred-thousand souls in attendance were already well aware, along with the rest of England, that they were living the summer of their lives. In 300 years it had never been hotter; the festival was simply adding to an atmosphere of carnival. That night a relentless Mick Jagger graced the giant tongue-shaped stage until two in the morning. By the time a series of storms arrived a few days later to break the heat, that summer was firmly enshrined in the collective consciousness as one of mythic idyll to which all subsequent summers would be compared. There have been serious heatwaves since - 1995 was technically drier, and 2003 more deadly - but none that have challenged '76 in the national memory.

Until this year. Marked by World Cup delirium, political turmoil and a six week spell of parched Mediterranean days, the summer of 2018 was this generation's singularly unforgettable season. Everywhere a sense of riotous fun took hold, a generosity of spirit, a welcome reversal of life's old order. Temperatures were so extreme that visiting Greeks and Spaniards, normally amused by the glee with which the English greet their meagre annual allotment of sunshine, wilted with us in the heat. Festival weekends played out in record highs instead of the usual mud baths, a penalty shootout ended in triumph. It even became possible to make friends on the Tube.

Perhaps nowhere else on earth is the character of a nation so utterly transformed by a simple string of hot days. And this change is so pronounced precisely because England's temperate climate and infamously grey skies have been its very destiny. In *The Remains of the Day* Kazuo Ishiguro notes, via his narrator Stevens, that the greatness of the English landscape, and by extension the greatness of its people, lies not in extraordinary vistas but in "the very lack of obvious drama or spectacle." It's a quaint and mawkish sentiment - that English sensibility is defined above all by restraint of the heart - but one proved at least partly true by the way in which, when the sun finally does come out, we lose our effing minds.

In *Playtime* Orlando Gili captures the ardour of an ancient nation in its rare and perfect summer days. His portraits shimmer with mischief and impulse - suddenly all is permitted. They evoke, too, a sense of endlessness. Framed in brazen colour the men, women, boys and girls seem to say, *maybe autumn will never come again, maybe I'll never age another day*. At last England's corseted soul is set loose; after the gloom, now the joy.

Henley Royal Regatta

Noisily Festival

Notting Hill Carnival

VE Weekend, Royal Gunpowder Mills

Glyndebourne Festival

Royal Wedding, Prince Harry and Meghan Markle, Hampshire Street Party

AT LAND'S END

Introduction by Adam Woodward & Photographs by Liz Seabrook

English Islands have long held a special place in our collective imagination. They are the settings of grand literary adventures and open-skied escapism, far-flung locations where time slows and the England of yesteryear remains perfectly preserved. These outposts, be they lesser-known or well-trodden, offer an enticing blend of culture, history and nature, attracting surfers, sunbathers and bird-watchers alike - and for a few days spread out over the course of a sweltering summer, we decided to join them.

Situated in the Bristol Channel, 12 miles from the Devon coast, Lundy is a grass-blanketed granite outcrop steeped in folklore and heritage. Despite evidence of human activity dating back 4,000 years, the island is virtually unspoiled, save for a 13th century castle and church, a tavern and a clutch of holiday cottages. The main reason: the most common seasonal visitors are not people but seabirds, with the island's rugged westerly cliffs making it prime real estate for nesting guillemots, Manx shearwaters and puffins. As one of the only parts of the UK frequented by the latter, you might expect Lundy to be swarming with eager twitchers jostling for the best vantage point, but the island has a refreshingly relaxed, unfussy vibe. It's also one of those rare destinations where getting there is half the fun - Lundy is served by its own passenger ship, the MS Oldenburg, of which dolphins and seals appear particularly enamoured.

The second, not-quite-as-quaint stop on our tour was the Isle of Sheppey, which is connected to Kent's northern coastline by a sweeping road bridge and populated by some 40,000 people. Having driven across from the mainland, we arched around to the island's most south-easterly point, where one of two National Nature Reserves shelters rare species of butterfly and waterfowl. On the way back we stopped off in Sheerness, a commercial port and decaying seaside town which, whilst not being the prettiest patch in the Garden of England, remains a popular retreat for Londoners, thanks largely to its long shingle beach.

Our final day trip took us to arguably the most quintessential of England's islands, the Isle of Wight. We stayed at Haven Hall, a charming, privately owned residence on the outskirts of Shanklin. This renovated Victorian mansion boasts landscaped gardens, an outdoor pool, lawn tennis court and spectacular views across the English Channel - not to mention a resident labradoodle named Maisie.

Waking at dawn the following morning, we made for the iconic Alum Bay and adjoining Needles, before stopping for lunch at The Garlic Farm on the edge of the downs (their garlic-infused beer and ice-cream come highly recommended). After a quick dip at Compton Bay, a quiet locals' spot with a decent break for surfing, we went searching for red squirrels at Borthwood Copse. The island's most famous inhabitants are evidently less assertive than their grey cousins but this dense area of ancient woodland is well worth exploring all the same. Similarly historic is St Catherine's Oratory, which was built by the Lord of Chale in 1328 as penance for stealing several casks of wine from a nearby shipwreck. Also known as the Pepperpot, the surviving tower stands on one of the island's highest points, offering a dramatic panoramic perspective.

Each of these islands has its own distinct characteristics but collectively they capture something of the essence of Englishness, revealing its storied past as well as its unique quirks and contradictions.

havenhall.uk
visitisleofwight.co.uk

FRUITS OF THE FOREST

Words by Liz Schaffer & Illustrations by Piera Cirefice

Fine fare and open spaces.

The folklore-filled New Forest is a wild wonderland, a collage of heath, woods, heather and gorse, an England of old. A landscape of dense greenwood, stone villages and moorland akin to the open, weather-beaten expanses of the north. Oaks, yews and elms grow madly, bent every which way in their search for sunlight and space, while the ground is spongy underfoot, softened by moss and decades of fallen leaves. All around bees buzz, at home in this rare and beguiling sylvan sphere.

The New Forest was created in 1079 as royal hunting grounds for William the Conqueror, and is today classified as 'ancient semi-natural woodland' - a type of terrain once common but which now only covers two percent of England. Living up to its name, the forest we encounter today is younger than one might expect - for the most part only around 350 years old - the region having been shaped by centuries of farming and industry. However, it's not just arboreal marvels that lure visitors to the region. There is, in fact, a quiet foodie revolution unfolding here, with hotels like Lime Wood, The Montagu Arms and Chewton Glen tempting gourmands. Come for the wilderness, stay for the flavour.

And so it was the promise of fine fare and muddy paths that saw my partner and I make for Brockenhurst, hiring bikes from Cyclexperience to get better acquainted with the region. In this, we were aided by their maps, which guide riders along the various routes meandering through the national park, and offer two touring options for those who prefer a 'fast' or 'pondering' pace.

Conveniently, our inaugural expedition led straight to our first hotel, Balmer Lawn, found beside a tawny creek where children leapt from bridges and banks, shaded by branches heavy with apples, blackberries and sloes. Fittingly, this modern, spacious abode could not be more family-oriented. Like much in the area, things feel welcoming here - tramping gear is *de rigueur*, the outdoor pool glimmers, their relaxed restaurant serves exceptional British classics and all around the forest beckons. Well-marked trails lead out from Balmer Lawn, or the daring can forge their own, bolstering the work of wanderers past by adding fallen branches to makeshift tepees dotted between the trees. The landscape changes fast, from forest, to meadow, to heath, to quaint villages where ponies halt traffic and gardens are guarded by stone walls and cattle grids - although the fight to protect foliage from peckish bovine neighbours appears futile.

Resuming our cycle, we called in at Le Blaireau, an organic French restaurant where the interiors - a mix of floral tiles and ornate iron work - evoke the Deco splendour of Parisienne bistros, and then proceeded to the garden of the delightfully lopsided Thatched Cottage Hotel (constructed in 1627) for scones and gin.

Yet our culinary escapades really began in Beaulieu, a charming town filled with moss-adorned stone houses, tea shops and ancient mills, and home to The Montagu Arms, a historic hotel in the Pride of Britain collection. A coaching inn has stood on this site since the 16th century, in various guises, and its curious past no doubt added weight to Sir Arthur Conan Doyle's attempt to banish a disgruntled spirit from the nearby Beaulieu Estate. Charles de Gaulle also stayed here during the Second World War, as did the Home Guard, who made use of many of the New Forest's stately homes.

Rooms are spread across the main house, cottages and the cocooning Hay Loft Suites, which are found in what were once the crumbling stables. However, the star attraction is the 3AA Rosette Terrace Restaurant, with its wood panelling, gilt mirrors and tapestry-like carpet depicting the animals of the New Forest. This is the domain of chef Matthew Tomkinson, a Roux Scholar who has been with the hotel for over a decade. His dishes - best sampled as part of a surprise tasting menu - are a fascinating fusion of French extravagance and British home cooking, and utilise Hampshire and Dorset produce, as well as ingredients from the hotel's Kitchen Garden - a cornucopia of herbs and vegetables adored by local cows and donkeys.

Having justly overindulged on Tomkinson's creations (and paired wines), I awoke the next morning in need of a wander, so followed a stone path from the hotel to the Solent Way. My small section of the 60 mile walk shadowed the river, snaking past sun-warmed meadows, bracken, long-abandoned brickyards and drink stations policed by honesty boxes, to Bucklers Hard. This sleepy hamlet was created as a port for to the West Indies sugar trade. However, as the French assumed control of the islands before its completion, it instead became a boat building hub. It was here that the HMS Agamemnon was constructed, immortalised in the Battle of Trafalgar.

Should you crave more foodie extravagance, spend some time at Lime Wood, a Georgian home-turned-luxury-hotel found outside the village of Lyndhurst. Bordered by undulating purple heath and immaculately landscaped gardens, it is here that you'll find Hartnett Holder & Co, a revered, light-filled restaurant from Angela Hartnett (who worked under Gordon Ramsay at Aubergine) and Luke Holder. Its walls are bedecked with an eclectic array of artwork, a melange of different periods and printmaking techniques. And while the space is undeniably grand, with high ceilings, teardrop light features and statement furniture, everything remains calm and welcoming. This is largely thanks to the wine list (made up of over 700 varieties) and the Tuscany-meets-New Forest menu.

Hartnett Holder & Co dishes are best when shared and the flavour combinations are both unexpected and faultless - think pickled vegetables served alongside the creamiest of ewe's cheese, and polenta-filled ravioli finished with peas. Courses appear upon custom-made plates (nods to the ornate vintage crockery of yesteryear) and with Hampshire's natural larder guiding the menu, it's unlikely two meals will ever be quite the same. However, a constant showstopper emerges in 'The Forest Floor', a dessert constructed from every conceivable type of chocolate - a gastronomic ode to the sun-dappled, lichenous, chaotic magic of the New Forest.

"

*A constant showstopper emerges
in 'The Forest Floor', a dessert
constructed from every conceivable type
of chocolate - a gastronomic ode to the
sun-dappled, lichenous, chaotic magic
of the New Forest.*

"

Equally dedicated to local produce and artistry is Chewton Glen, a family-friendly, old world country hotel with heart. The design is stunning; traditional with a touch of the fantastic. There is retro wallpaper and ornate plasterwork, a central staircase made for dramatic entrances and a book-lined, Burgundy-hued bar where portraits, mirrors and *objets d'art* adorn every surface. The rooms are sizeable yet snug - unique, luxurious abodes that become yours the moment you enter. And then there's the spa, which is so divine that minds roam and dozing off is wholeheartedly encouraged - as is combining treatments like a Himalayan salt and oil scrub with time in the hydrotherapy pool, the largest in Europe.

Chewton Glen was the preferred bolthole (then a family home) of Captain Frederick Marryat, author of *The Children of the New Forest*, a classic tale set during the English Civil War. And while it's easy to suspect that the sprawling grounds, which come complete with a walled garden and orchard, have changed little since Marryat's visits, I doubt he feasted on anything as spectacular as the meals served in Chewton Glen's Dining Room. Indeed, at dinner I was so distracted by my partner's euphoria as he ate delicate, silky oysters the size of my palm - "the king of oysters," he exclaimed - that I almost forgot the brilliance of my own scallops … *almost.*

The seafood served here is sublime - Thai lobster curry, dressed Devonshire crab, wild sea bass, South Coast cod - largely because the ingredients don't travel all that far. Amble past the hotel's outdoor pool, across the croquet lawn and through the golf course - pausing to admire Bruce Denny's sculptures - and you'll find a path. This leads to a 'bunny' (a wooded ravine once popular with New Forest smugglers), the remains of Chewton Mill, through forest filled with hazel and holly, and on to the pebbled expanse of Highcliffe and Barton-on-Sea. Here Solent and sky merge to form a thrilling blue expanse whilst the Isle of Wights's cliffs glow on the horizon. The walk, one that leads to an entirely new, dazzling world, takes a mere 20 minutes. An enchanting reminder that New Forest landscapes are prone to shifting with little warning. Which is what draws so many to this protected patch of southern wilderness; a long-adored natural playground where culinary offerings are exceptional, hotels are hives of history and character, and life unfolds at a calmer pace. It is a region entirely its own - ever-evolving, riotous and utterly bewitching.

chewtonglen.com
prideofbritainhotels.com/hotels/the-montagu-arms
limewoodhotel.co.uk
thenewforest.co.uk

-Montagu Arms-

-panage season-

-Chewton Glen-

-Nightjar-

LAKELAND TRAILS

Words by Dan Richards & Photographs by Simon Bray & Robin Forster

Impressions from trips to Wastwater, Ullswater and various summits.

Lingmell, the morning of my third day in the Lakes. Buff heather scrub and hummocky grasses underfoot, the long drag up, the bunched gorse and gathering heat in my legs, the prickly sweat, the view back over Wastwater to the coaly screes and then, eventually, reaching the summit, swathed in mizzle. And then, better still, the prospect of Lingmell Gill, white in its flume, the muscular channel around it green rising through tan, bronze and coffee. Brown Tongue lolling underneath the Scafells' swollen sculpted bulk, reflected in Wastwater's deep green shellac.

It was a great feeling to be standing there, alone - overlooking and overlooked in equal measure. I'd grown up with the stories of this place; my childhood home was chock-full of books and art steeped in this landscape, reflecting its wild aspect - Romantics and visionaries, Blake, Coleridge, De Quincey, Scott and Potter. I could delve into shared memory here, shared personal and national acquaintance: English classes and 'Daffodils', that small hand-me-down *Peter Rabbit*; journeys up Shap to see university friends in Aberdeen or cousins in Edinburgh - leaving Bristol Temple Meads at dawn, the run of Preston, Lancaster, Oxenholme Lake District "change for trains to Windermere", and Carlisle; motorway dozing in our old Saab on family holidays.

One of my earliest memories, blurred at the edges, a Polaroid third person vision, is of a trip to Brathay Hall in Ambleside. I must have been almost three. My mother, Annie, went for a nap after the long drive up the M6 so my father, Tim, took me out for a row on the lake, my small hands dragging in the water.

"It's really funny, the way you eat like a pig!" I cheerfully told a man with a beard at the dinner table next to me that night, apparently. I followed this up the next day, in a loud voice clearly audible to the kitchen staff, with "isn't it funny how we've had tomatoes for every meal?"

"We bundled you out of the room and went for fish and chips," remembers Annie, "You were so funny. At one point you said to Tim, 'I wonder if people get fed up with all this water?' and he tried to rationalise it and explain that that was the wonderful thing about the place, what all the tourists came for. 'Look at the mountains,' he said, 'look at all the mountains.' 'And the water,' you said. 'It's everywhere!'" I was clearly a very astute child.

Driving in the Lakes all these years later, over the Hardknott Pass - the vehicular acme of a landscape I'd seen building since the Bowland Fells - I wound down a road which veered, meandered and dropped through the rust and umber bracken like a bored child's finger on a fogged car window - a silver thread shining in the rain, soundtracked by an engine in low gear.

Around Cockley Beck, before the incline arrows started massing on the map, I stopped beside the River Duddon to take some photographs. The surface of the river was pitted with rain. The patter and swish of water filled my ears, but even sodden it was beautiful; craggy orange slopes rose at my back, bogs sprung underfoot, the rich hay of ferns, the shallow, rapid river. As so often on the trip, I was the only person there, standing in the streaming air, soaking it up.

With characteristic humour and sincere enthusiasm, my great-great aunt, Dorothea Pilley, once wrote that the landscape around Wasdale allows "that connoisseurship which finds that the mountains are never on two days alike" to be exercised to the full. "The relative delights of degrees of wateriness could be tasted! The difference between 'A wet day' and 'wet all day and *very wet*' properly appreciated."

I slept one night at Burnthwaite Farm, a National Trust B&B at the head of the Wasdale Pass. The first morning was beautifully misted, bitter and

blowing. I set out towards Great Gable along Moses Trod, the 17th century packhorse route over Sty Head that passes through the farm. Walking into the V between Lingmell and Gable, the scale of the slopes became apparent. To my mind Wasdale is a vague relation of Aviemore in Scotland, a distant cousin of Interlaken and Arolla in Switzerland in terms of its position as a jumping-off point - a base within the mountains from which to set about the several-hundred-metre peaks above; and about a half mile from the farm I began to do just that, ascending the grass snoot of Great Gable's southwest corner, the long green grind of Gavel Neese.

From the icy moonland summit I looked across to Lingmell, rising from its taupe base to frosted top. The day before I'd tramped up the matted slopes below Stand Crag and Criscliffe Knotts - tussocks and quag, clothes wring-wet, Piers Ghyll deepening into a vast cleft down to my left. Over the canyon, sheep stood chewing, perched on outcrops, indifferent and blank. Teetering on a precipice clearly didn't put the Herdwick off their lunch. I'd eaten a piece of tea bread in solidarity and shortly after crossed an invisible line where rain became sleet.

Later that night, eating stew at the Wasdale Inn, I noted how the staff all seemed to be young, a mix of walkers, climbers and fell runners, who either grew up nearby or were drawn from afar by the prospect of work in Wasdale and the chance to explore the District on their days off.

The third or fourth morning in the area. Walking out past the yews huddled around St. Olaf's Church, I saw one of the inn workers setting off straight up the slope of Kirk Fell, alone, through the bracken and red ferns, head down, set on her path. I could still make her out when I reached Mosedale Bridge - high on the fell, looking back over Wastwater toward the sea - and I thought *what an amazing place this must be to live, work and wake within each day.* Perhaps she was thinking the same that moment before she turned away and disappeared into the clouds.

The last day, sunshine, cycling down the deep, dappled lanes to Ullswater - a mirror between green steeps, cupped glass. The night before I'd stayed with Luxury Lodges Whitbarrow, an indulgent outlier amidst the granite, moss and silver birch. Stargazing in their outside tub, chill Milky Way spilling into bubble bath fizz - a decadent memory which now mixes with the wake of My Lady of the Lake, most historic of the famous Ullswater Steamers.

Leaving my bike at Pooley Bridge, I'd hopped aboard the handsome vessel, dazzling in teal, cream and red. Built in 1877, she's reputed to be the oldest working passenger ferry in the world. As we spun towards Glenridding, the boat a stately arrow beneath a cloudless sky, I leant on the rail and thought of Tim and I splashing about in our little boat.
"Look at the mountains," he'd said, "look at all the mountains."
"And the water," I'd said. "It's everywhere!"

Editor's Note: Dan spent his last few Lake District nights with Luxury Lodges in their sweeping, homely and brilliantly designed self-catering 'Farmhouse Collection' apartment. Surrounded by fields, quizzical sheep and farm shops - and only a short cycle from Ullswater (bikes, supplies and local knowledge available on request) - this delightful three-bedroom apartment claims the top floor of a converted farmhouse in the Whitbarrow grounds, and boasts a private terrace, thoroughly English wallpaper and statement soft furnishings one longs to steal away.

luxurylodges.com

DARK SKIES

Words & Photographs by Jim Johnston

Looking to the heavens.

Time spent beneath bright stars and dark skies can lead to more questions than answers. If there was a Big Bang, what came before? If the Universe is still growing, then how small was it when it all began? What lies in wait beyond those distant galaxies? Are we alone? No, surely not! These are just a few of the mind-boggling thoughts that spring forward when standing in an ancient landscape below a quiet, bright, immeasurable cosmos. I doubt I will ever fully grasp the rules and theories that govern the skies above - or find the answers to my musings - but I will always enjoy the sense of perspective, the feeling of simultaneous insignificance and connectivity, that looking up at the stars inspires.

Only 22 percent of England has pristine night skies untouched by light pollution and you need to travel even further, escaping the lingering glow of towns and motorways, to find skies that are truly dark. Once you are under them though, you're immediately aware that you've reached the far, wild reaches of the English countryside, places where you're firmly rooted in the present, even if the wonders overhead are billions of years old. Bright stars are a key characteristic of rural areas and the celestial displays of these stygian locations promise adventure, retreat and ample opportunity to slow down and look up. Stargazers here can observe 50 times more stars than they would in a major town or city, the world above complex, hypnotic and enthralling.

Of the darkest measured skies in England, over half are in national parks and Areas of Outstanding Natural Beauty, and these places play a vital role in protecting and enhancing our experience of the countryside. Increasingly, national parks are taking proactive steps to fight light pollution, promoting off-season visitation (the clarity of a cloudless winter night is spellbinding) and protecting nocturnal habitats in the process.

Exmoor National Park is a pioneering example of what can be achieved in terms of conservation when working in partnership with local landowners, businesses and individuals. Bridging the southwest counties of Devon and Somerset, the core of this dark sky reserve covers an area of approximately 83 square kilometres and within it, the National Park Authority has developed a strong lighting policy to limit light pollution. It became the first International Dark Sky Reserve in Europe in 2011 and hosts an annual Dark Skies Discovery Festival with an ever-expanding line-up of nocturnal events and activities.

As part of these festivities, I joined a night swim in the peaty waters of Pinkery Pond, an artificial lake formed 200-odd years ago, found just east of the village of Challacombe. Guided by Channel Adventure, a bubbly neoprene-clad group of daring swimmers and I excitedly slipped into the mirror-like moorland lake as night fell. There were already thousands of stars visible to the naked eye but we had to wait a short while until the marvels of the Universe could be appreciated in full. Despite the magnitude of what was slowly revealing itself above, more pressing matters - such as the freezing autumnal waters and mysterious shadows moving beneath the black surface - continued to demand our attention. But then our wetsuits warmed up, the nervous laughter subsided and we became lost in the Elysian experience, floating on our backs and holding hands in silence while looking up at the constellations and wispy noctilucent clouds. The haze of the Milky Way - its presence the marker of 'dark sky' - appeared in glowing detail, the spectacle so astounding that it was difficult to appreciate the fact that what we were seeing was no longer there. These stars are so distant that when looking at them we are essentially gazing back through time, their light taking eons to finally reach us.

> *But then our wetsuits warmed up, the nervous laughter subsided and we became lost in the Elysian experience, floating on our backs and holding hands in silence while looking up at the constellations and wispy noctilucent clouds.*

For those who prefer stargazing on dry land, telescopes can be hired from National Park Centres and several accommodation providers host regular stargazing and astronomical talks. Run in partnership with The Forestry Commission, a guided night-time wildlife walk is another excellent way to experience dark skies, learn about the nocturnal environment and find Polaris, the marker of true north - hooting barn owls and the occasional grunting stag adding atmosphere on the near silent moors.

Much further north you'll find the darkest area in England - the Northumberland International Dark Sky Park (NIDSP), the largest area of protected night sky in Europe. NIDSP covers the entire Northumberland National Park and 67 percent of Kielder Water and Forest Park, totalling nearly 1,483 square kilometres. Northumberland National Park has developed local lighting guidance to ensure that no new light pollution is created in the area, protecting the stars above and the landscape below, making it a haven for both professional and amateur astronomers. The region caters for all levels of comfort too, from a bivvy bag on the ground looking up with budget binoculars, to a calming stay at the welcoming Battlesteads Hotel in Wark. The hotel, found in what was once a farmhouse, has its own observatory adjacent to its restaurant, and ending an evening of locally sourced Northumbrian food with a spot of Aurora hunting, glass of wine in hand, is certainly one way to congratulate yourself on a day well spent. Courses and longer night photography workshops are available through the hotel for those wishing to further develop their astronomical skills.

The Sill's National Landscape Discovery Centre is another well-equipped venue if you're keen to stay and stargaze in Northumberland. Found in the shadow of Hadrian's Wall, the centre offers a programme of events alongside interactive displays and exhibits - like one allowing visitors to detect meteors using radio astronomy - all designed to educate and help protect some of England's most pristine locations.

Darkness can have a profound effect on people's experience of a landscape and the night remains a crucial resource. But as cities expand and we spend increasing amounts of time indoors, we have somehow lost that deep connection with the Universe that defined so much of our collective history. England's dark skies are an amazing spectacle and, whilst a little effort is required to reach them, the country's relatively small size means you are never that far from a memorable, star-filled encounter. Beyond the glow of the tame, built and familiar lies an entirely different England - a place where you can ask yourself the big questions, without ever really expecting an answer.

> *I doubt I will ever fully grasp the rules and theories that govern the skies above - or find the answers to my musings - but I will always enjoy the sense of perspective, the feeling of simultaneous insignificance and connectivity, that looking up at the stars inspires.*

Dark Sky Discovery
darkskydiscovery.org.uk

Channel Adventure
channeladventure.co.uk

West Withy Farm Cottages
exmoor-cottages.com

The Sill -
National Landscape Discovery Centre
thesill.org.uk

Battlesteads Hotel & Restaurant
battlesteads.com

FANTASTIC BEASTS AND WHERE TO FIND THEM

Words by Dan Richards & Photographs by Liz Schaffer

A Jurassic Coast itinerary from Imbarc, a travel and culture website dedicated to escape.

From the Purbeck Ridge above Tyneham, just before the road wheels sharply down towards the village of Steeple, one is afforded a marvellous view over the leaf-spring chalk downs to the sea. Over the next rise, hidden for now, lies the parish of Kimmeridge - famed for its fossils and eponymous clay, laid down in the late or upper Jurassic. The village is home to a world renowned reliquiae, a hard-pressed menagerie of turtles and ammonites, barnacles and crocodiles; sauropods, plesiosaurs, pliosaurs, ichthyosaurs and many other toothy monsters - but more of that later. For now, we drive on, up and down the ripple hills, drifting through green atop hidden white ribs.

We're staying at Smedmore House, one of Dorset's finest Georgian manors and a property admired and selected by Imbarc, who have curated our journey. A handsome house of Portland stone, Smedmore's balanced, open face greets us as we crunch onto the drive. Once inside, the building reveals itself to have eight bedrooms spread over several rambling floors, at the centre of which sits a large wooden staircase overseen by family portraits and oil paintings of game birds and hunting scenes in styles akin to Henri Rousseau - *Pheasant in a Tropical Storm or Surprised!*

The room in which we sleep looks out over the distant bay; a large, light boudoir of soft cottons and silks. A Bloomsbury feel, an airy Charleston chamber beyond which roll baize lawns and mysterious woods full of sphinxes, urns and obelisks. Affectionally known as 'The Bridal Suite' in relation to the many weddings this most romantic of manors hosts throughout the year, the bedroom gives off onto a long corridor lined with maps and sea charts. Smedmore abounds in art and cultural riches from around the world, each possessed of unique story and provenance. Downstairs there are high-ceilinged salons full of Chinese ceramics and Dutch furniture dating from the 1690s, together with a chair used by Napoleon whilst imprisoned on Saint Helena, land deeds and seals dating back to the dawn of wax. There is also a small museum of the tremendous acts of heroism and nursing care conducted in the First World War by relations of Smedmore's current owner, historian Dr Philip Mansel, a direct descendant of William Wyot who bought the house over 600 years ago.

The next morning, having explored the manor's flower gardens and walled orchards, communed with muzzy bees and feckless pheasants, and sauntered down pine avenues fuggy with frankincense, we catch sight of the distant form of Clavell Tower, a folly like a black rook overlooking Kimmeridge Bay.

In 2008, the tower was saved from ruin, painstakingly moved back stone by stone from its yawning cliff edge perch and restored on a new

> *The next morning, having explored the manor's flower gardens and walled orchards, communed with muzzy bees and feckless pheasants, and sauntered down pine avenues fuggy with frankincense, we catch sight of the distant form of Clavell Tower.*

foundation. It is now the Landmark Trust's most popular property and the waiting list to stay in its lighthouse-like interior is long. The bay below was once the haunt of smugglers and the scene of many a skirmish between ne'er-do-wells and coast guards in the 17th and 18th centuries. The next cove along to the west, a shallow shingled crescent, is named Brandy Bay in a nod to the stealthy contraband skulduggery that went on before Clavell Tower's time. The folly provides an excellent position from which to inspect the striated peninsular, a layer-cake of shale, Portland stone and sand and clay which has made the area such a mecca for fossil enthusiasts. As well as being profoundly green and pleasant on the eye, the land here is unique in its geological make up - a fact recognised by its multi-gong status as a UNESCO World Heritage Site, Area of Outstanding Natural Beauty and Site of Special Scientific Interest. For whilst it is dubbed the Jurassic Coast, the 95 miles of seashore which extends from Studland in Purbeck to Exmouth in Devon, features rocks from the Triassic and Cretaceous eras too. According to the Royal Geographical Society, it's the only place on earth where 185 million years of geological history are sequentially exposed in cliffs, coves, stacks and barrier beaches.

Back inland we visit The Etches Collection, the life's work of a remarkable man: renowned amateur palaeontologist, Steve Etches MBE. This new museum in the heart of Kimmeridge acts as treasure house, workshop and village hall; a museum in which the creatures uncovered and amassed by Etches can be viewed and contextualised, and a space for the man himself to clean, restore and classify his amazing archive.

Further up the coast, Lulworth Cove is another port of call for tourists and geology enthusiasts, although the goal here is arguably less subtle than the delicate undulating coaly beasties which so animate Etches.

Most have come to see the giant hag stone of Durdle Door - an immense oolite arch of a shape that puts me in mind of a dragon, a flexuous Nessie. 'Durdle' is derived from the Old English word *thirl*, meaning bore or drill, and indeed the sea has hollowed the most theatrical vault. When the water is calm the reflection forms an uncanny ellipse of sky. Swimmers pass through the magic portal. Children splash on the shore. Dogs run about half mad with glee. Away in the distance the woomph and ratter-tat of the Lulworth firing range recalls a world beyond these cliffs and sets my stomach rumbling in solidarity. Time for lunch.

Dorset is a county packed with excellent restaurants with a strong belief in sustainability and local produce. Guided by Imbarc, we eat very well during our stay and polish off a lot of fish. Rick Stein's new outpost in Sandbanks was the venue for a wonderful supper of Dover sole and blonde ray; the former deboned at the table in a mesmeric flash of moves, the latter's butter flesh an utter delight with the result that the fine fan skeleton was soon combed clean. Earlier, when I'd asked from where our oyster starters hailed, our maître d' had smiled and gestured out towards the blues and bobbing boats of Poole Harbour.

But for lunch after Lulworth - Durdle dins, if you will - we make for The Pig on the Beach in Studland Bay, two miles north of Swanage, skirting the iconic white headland which tails into Old Harry Rocks by means of deep lanes spun green. The Pig's menus feature an illustrated map of where their ingredients are grown and bred. Their aim is to source everything from the Dorset and Devon surrounds (or else have a special relationship with small suppliers) and plates with names like Studland spider crab pappardelle, pressed Piddle Valley chicken, Jurassic Coast cuttlefish and James Golding's home smoked Loch Duart salmon attest to their efforts in this area. Kitchen gardens set in wildflower meadows add further pep and freshness and our sommelier is at charming pains to match our meal to his cellar, taking the trouble to explain both his thinking and the provenance of each wine proffered.

Back in Swanage, mid afternoon, fortified and giddy from our crackling lunch, we totter aboard a simmering steam train which travels along the restored branch line from Wareham. It is one of the region's great tourism success stories and a dazzling labour of love for the volunteers who operate the locomotives and maintain the stock, stations and track. As we run down the backs of houses and out into the cow-loud countryside, stopping at halts rebuilt to be forever between the wars, it is easy to lose oneself in Dorset's pastoral charm - but through the drifts of smoke ahead there appears the ghost of Corfe Castle, a reminder of darker days of battles, treachery and dissolution.

An American friend once commented that England and the 'eccentric English' love to hang on to their history and 'play it back' all at once. Corfe Castle is surely an exemplar of this. We alight from our 20s train, opposite a signal box from 1885 (restored in 2012), in the shadow of an 11th century castle built by William the Conqueror, and wander through an enchanting village beloved of Enid Blyton and a central location in *Bedknobs and Broomsticks*. All we need are some Morris Dancers to appear, a Roman Legion to be camped on the

Victorian church steps and a Spitfire flypast to complete the picture.

The monolithic castle ruins are a truly striking sight. High, massed and smashed on its flinty chalk tump, even broken into massive blocks it gives a magnificent sense of power and heft. Alfred the Great built the first castle from wood on a hill formed where two streams had eroded a gap in the long chalk ridge where we stood at the start of this article. The fort's purpose was to put the willies up any would-be Danish invaders and things tootled along relatively sensibly for a few hundred years until, on the 18th March 978, King Edward the Martyr's reign was brutally cut short; a stabbing in the back possibly ordered by his stepmother, Queen Æthelflæd of Mercia - 'as highborn as she was beautiful' - so her own Æthelred (the Unready) could ascend to the throne. Dark stuff!

Throughout the medieval period Corfe was a royal castle. After the Battle of Hastings a Norman structure replaced the wooden Saxon keep, the splintered remains of which still stand, witness to Corfe Castle's final throws - destroyed at the behest of Parliament after the Civil War. Another awesome leviathan in the Jurassic Coast's marvellous bestiary.

Dan's dazzling Dorset tour was arranged by Imbarc, a luxury travel company and website for worldly wanderers, awe-seeking adventurers and creative thinkers. Imbarc curate bespoke itineraries to a range of international and UK destinations based on their client's specific needs and interests, arranging transport, tours, hotels and restaurants.

imbarc.co.uk

"

High, massed and smashed on its flinty chalk tump, even broken into massive blocks it gives a magnificent sense of power and heft.

"

TO THE WALL

Words & Photographs by Joel Clifton

A journey along the Roman frontier.

In 120 A.D. the Roman Emperor Hadrian began the construction of a wall in Britannia, designed to consolidate the Empire's lands and protect its citizens from the unconquerable wilds to the north. Stretching for 80 miles across modern-day England, it stood sentinel for centuries and remains the largest intact Roman artefact on the planet. A thing of awe and wonder, travellers have long been enticed to the wall, not only to connect with history but to explore the land it stands upon, one of the last wild corners of England, an enduring natural frontier. Hearing about Hadrian's Cycleway, a route that follows the structure from coast to coast, incorporating a vast network of forested trails, winding gravel roads and cobblestone lanes, I too couldn't resist the allure of Hadrian's Wall.

To experience a country by bicycle is a wonderful thing. You breathe deeper, think slower and find your senses heightened. You notice more - birds in the trees and the rhythms of waterways - and remain in complete control, free to stop whenever and wherever you choose. But, most importantly, you also feel every mile, working your body as you push and pull yourself through a landscape, appreciating its nuances all the more in the process.

The River Tyne was to be my guide along Hadrian's Cycleway, leading me past rolling farmland, deciduous forests, open fields and the occasional medieval village, and flying into Newcastle from Toronto, I couldn't wait to begin. However, upon collecting my hired bike and gear from The Cycle Hub, a cafe popular with Newcastle's cycling community, I was promptly reminded that, when it comes to cycling and the great outdoors, things don't always go to plan.

This was never meant to be a physically challenging trip, more of a relaxing cruise across the countryside with regular stops for photography, food, scenery appreciation and history. And Hadrian's Cycleway certainly can be leisurely, unless you accidentally plan to ride from Newcastle to a farm in the Pennines in one day, on a touring bike, carrying a week's worth of kit. I was set to stay at The Cowshed (one of the stunning, character-packed holiday homes in the Crabtree & Crabtree portfolio), yet halfway through my second Cycle Hub latte I realised I'd entered the wrong postcode when plotting my route. My four hour cycle had turned into an 11 hour expedition - and it was already 10 a.m.

About two hours out of Newcastle you begin to sense the romance of the English landscape. The streets narrow, the woods thicken and the buildings become fairy tale cottages. After five hours, you reach Corbridge, a charming village that was once

> *The River Tyne was to be my guide along Hadrian's Cycleway, leading me past rolling farmland, deciduous forests, open fields and the occasional medieval village.*

the northernmost settlement of the Roman Empire. Found beside the Tyne, its stone bridge was built in 1674 as an earlier version had fallen victim to border warfare. Refuelling at The Angel of Corbridge, I felt I'd arrived in the England of my imagination. From the inn's patio I could see down the rise and over tightly-pitched roofs to the bridge and up into the rolling hills beyond.

I wish I had given myself more time, because the ride from Corbridge to The Cowshed is spectacular. The road winds through craggy hills and farmland, where sheep graze between small lakes and stone walls. It's here that you'll find the highest point of the cycleway, the summit marked by a steel cairn labelled with the distances from Wallsend in Newcastle to Wallsend in Bowness-On-Solway. Most people take two or three days to reach this marker, and here I was, a little more than halfway through day one, feeling the burn in my legs as the rain clouds rolled in.

At 11 p.m., in the black of a wet and windy night, I arrived at The Cowshed and, walking in, found all my pain and exhaustion immediately forgotten. The renovated, three bedroom, 400 year old barn feels like a haven, centred around a cosy living room where an ancient map of the region hangs above a deep, comfortable couch. In the fridge were vegetables, fruit, salmon, beer, cheese and eggs. I settled in, opened a bottle of Black Grouse Stout and, exhausted, became one with the couch.

The following morning, after a big mess of eggs, cheese and fresh bread, Neville Gill, the owner of The Cowshed, arrived to show me around his 1,000 acre farm. We explored the grouse butts his great-grandfather constructed for hunting and visited the 600 year old shepherd's cabin, high on a fell, which the Gill family still use during their annual grouse shoot. He showed me the trees he'd planted and the duck pond he'd dug and explained his future plans, all of which must pass stringent tests to ensure no undue damage is done to this antediluvian, interconnected environment - something Gill is passionate about.

As hard as it was to leave The Cowshed, I was excited to travel on, cycling west towards to sea. I peddled, photographed and slept deeply in Carlisle before continuing to Bowness-On-Solway, the scent of salt keeping me company along a narrow track, the aroma growing with every mile. In Bowness, I made for the Kings Arms, a pub which is built atop the remains of a Roman fort and was undergoing renovations during my visit. The cheerful woman behind the bar explained that everything was taking longer than expected as they'd unearthed historically significant remains, forcing them to stop work until the authorities weighed in. "That's just how it is here," she laughed. "You can't dig a hole in your yard without finding something important."

I considered this later on the shore of the Solway Firth, looking across the water to Scotland, struck by how lucky I was to be in such a fascinating, time-marked place. Here I could venture into the wild, swap stories with local farmers and pop into pubs in villages where the Romans had

> **"**
>
> *Hadrian's Wall wound its way, serpent-like, as far as the eye could see, across the landscape, following the natural line of the land.*
>
> **"**

ended their fortification lines and, even today, a column of marching soldiers wouldn't have looked out of place.

I felt similarly humbled at Sycamore Gap, where I'd come for a sunset view of the wall. Standing before the fortification, completely alone, I was amazed by its scale. Hadrian's Wall wound its way, serpent-like, as far as the eye could see, across the landscape, following the natural line of the land. The wall is now only three to four feet high, but during Roman rule it measured up to 20 feet - and that's on top of the rocky slope it sits above.

Keen to understand more about this structure, I paid a visit the following day to Vindolanda, the wall's largest Roman fortification and an active dig site overseen by Dr Andrew Birley. At least 30 volunteers were working away in the pit, a community of like-minded people, from all walks of life, for whom archaeology was not a profession but a passion. Everyone was chatting as they excavated, keen

to share tales of their discoveries, the thrill of seeing that first glint of light in the earth. Vindolanda has proven itself to be a rich source of artefacts and, despite decades of digging, Birley assures me they've only just scratched the surface.

I ended my journey by travelling backwards, to a village I'd been thinking about since first stopping there nearly a week ago. Corbridge and The Angel were as charming and picturesque as I remembered and I spent two days cradling pints and dipping my toes in the Tyne. This change of pace felt necessary, a way of calming the mind before returning to the modern world, the chance to think about those long-gone communities shaped by this fortification, and those drawn to it today. There are few places left where past and present remain so intertwined and the landscape is allowed to dominate. Perhaps this two-wheeled journey of mine should continue, I think, feet cooling in the river, for I sense there is so much more to uncover.

thecyclehub.org

crabtreeandcrabtree.com/properties/the-cowshed

ROGER DEAKIN'S SUFFOLK

Words by Joe Minihane
Illustrations by Marina Marcolin

Wild swimming and nature writing.

"There was a time for us too when Suffolk and the whole of the Waveney Valley was terra incognita, like the hills, woods and ponds around Thoreau's cabin at Walden."

Roger Deakin, *Notes from Walnut Tree Farm*

I walk across Outney Common, boots squelching through churned up mud, as a herd of cows throws me nonchalant glances from fifty paces. There's the caw of invisible ravens, the twirling song of a skylark, the silent wingbeats of a kestrel on high, watching something unseen in the tall grass.

I am here to swim in the Waveney, a river that arcs in a deep meander around this open space. It's late April and despite the spring sun burning off the dawn mist, a chill breeze lingers. Where the river forks and a row of timber steps are nailed into an overhanging horse chestnut, I slip into the cool water. Wavelets slap across my chest as I tack out into the deep, enjoying the frog's eye view. This is my favourite place, on the trail of a man who made this valley, this county, his home. A man whose writing gave rise to a new understanding of the natural world.

Roger Deakin was a swimmer, writer, woodsman, filmmaker and eccentric. He made his life at Walnut Tree Farm, a once-ruined Elizabethan farmhouse in the Suffolk village of Mellis. Surrounded by a medieval moat and acres of unkempt fields and woodland, it was a base for his adventures both local and far reaching.

In the years since his passing in 2006, Deakin and his works have become cornerstones of a resurgent nature writing scene in the UK. 1999's *Waterlog*, an ode to the delights of illicit swims in the country's hidden waterways, is now seen as totemic, kickstarting a wider appreciation of wild swimming. The posthumously released *Wildwood* revealed Deakin's deep knowledge of and adoration for forests and trees, such passions also evident in his diaries, released as *Notes from Walnut Tree Farm* in 2008.

My own connection to Deakin came through a shared love of wild swimming. *Waterlog* was, and still is, my bible. The author's impish sense of fun, love of flouting rules and understanding of the natural world spoke to me at a time when I was struggling with anxiety. I made it my mission to swim in all of the places Deakin had visited, a project which became my own book, *Floating*.

"The Waveney is a secret river, by turns lazy and agile, dashing over shallow beds of gravel, then suddenly quiet, dignified and deep."

Roger Deakin, *Waterlog*

In the three years since the end of my journey, I have missed diving into Deakin's world. Hence I am here, swimming in a pool on the Waveney that he described as "a perfect pike pool", all submerged tree roots and uneven banks. The water seems like the ideal way to see the world as Deakin did. He speaks of becoming part of the scene when swimming in rivers, of being at one with the creatures that make it their home, of gaining a sense of perspective unattainable on dry land.

From where I swim, the banks look impossibly high, the only sights a distant mansion and the course of the channel where it twists its way towards Bungay, Geldeston and the North Sea beyond. Low to the water, the breeze has dropped and the sun warms my back as I swim a lazy breaststroke. Deakin called this "the naturalists' stroke", all the better for the swimmer to see their surroundings. I can hear the whirr of goldfinches. The kestrel I saw earlier drops, hovers and drops again, rising once

more without prey. I picture pike hiding in the depths, waiting to bite, and make for the bank.

"This was the Wissey, a river so secret that even its name sounds like a whisper: a river of intoxicating beauty that appears to have avoided the late twentieth century altogether."

Roger Deakin, *Waterlog*

Across the county border, on the edge of Norfolk's sandy Brecklands, I follow the barbed wire fence of a MOD firing range. The late afternoon light is filtering through Scots pines and humanity seems to be elsewhere, disinterested, unaware of this spectacular little corner of England.

At a humpbacked bridge, where the paved road fades to dirt, the Wissey emerges from what Deakin called "the never never land" of the adjacent firing range, pouring into a swirling weir pool. I wade over slick, shelving pebbles into the white water, turn, and let its force ease out the knots in my back, before sliding into the shallows, willing myself to stay beneath the icy surface.

Because the firing range isn't troubled by intensive farming and agribusiness, the Wissey has retained a magical feel, that same "intoxicating beauty" Deakin observed 20 years ago. I wade out yet again as a tawny owl glides overhead. Deakin had an unerring ability to find and share sublime locations, especially those surrounding his Mellis moat. The fact that so many remain pristine feels like a rare gift, unchanging calm in the modern storm.

"I had come down the path along the disintegrating cliffs from the magnificent ruined church at Covehithe. Each year the path moves further inland across the fields because great hunks of England keep falling away in winter storms."

Roger Deakin, *Waterlog*

The light patter of April rain echoes inside my hood. I turn my back on the mossy walls of Covehithe Church and follow the path around farm fields to where small cliffs slip onto the sandy beach. It is late morning, the day after my blissful Wissey dip.

Covehithe is the fastest eroding stretch of English coastline with around five metres claimed by the sea each year. As storms continue to batter Suffolk every winter, it's likely the church and its 14th century ruins will be under the churning waves by the middle of the century.

Deakin writes in *Waterlog* of a ley line he drew from his moat to the coast just south of here. He stopped along its length to swim in pools near Eye and the lake in the grounds of Heveningham Hall. But instead I am drawn to this ethereal place, where Deakin swam in the now inaccessible Benacre Broad. Today, an electric fence tacked out around its perimeter protects ground-nesting birds. I walk along the beach, where fallen trees lay lop-sided, whitened by the sun, awaiting their futures as submarine habitats. As the rain intensifies, I give in to the water's call and run towards the roughed up rollers.

Turning to look back to the shore, I see my first swifts of the year, their unmistakable whistle catching on the growing wind. The waves rise and a sharp slap of salty water brings me back into the moment. "One of the beauties of this flat land of Suffolk is that when you're swimming off the shore and the waves come up, it subsides from view and you could be miles out in the North Sea," writes Deakin towards the end of *Waterlog*. I feel that here, now, and wish he was with me to enjoy the dip, to bob as a seal, to revel in the water and light he so hymned.

ARE WE THERE YET

- -

Introduction by Angela Terrell & Photographs by Tanya Houghton

————————

Few things are as liberating as a road trip; the sense of exploration and thrill of discovery growing as the miles amass. Maps dominate the dashboard, routes are altered on a whim and fickle English skies hold no sway. But add picture-perfect scenes filled with ruins mellowed by swathes of roses, peaceful villages with cobbled market squares and moorland dotted with black-faced sheep and, if you're a photography tragic (especially one venturing out solo), you may end up doing some rather slow touring.

This proved true when I embarked on a photographic jaunt through the Yorkshire Dales, the land of poets, artists and solitude, where a myriad of roads tracing through the idyllic landscape - glowing like silk ribbons in the morning sun or blanketed by cloud as rain threatened - provided ample opportunity to stop, absorb the gasp-worthy scenery and attempt to capture its splendour. It was always mildly surprising to actually reach my destination at the day's end, the incentives to travel onwards seemingly boundless.

Photographer Tanya Houghton set her image-collecting sights on Yorkshire's coastal beauty, following moss-covered drystone walls past farmyards and Dalby Forest's wooded grandeur towards the fossil-filled, seaweed-covered boulders of North York Moors National Park's shoreline. The coast here is stunning but constantly changing, eroding away, a victim of England's wild weather and waves. Clifftop paths reveal the drama of these stormy seas, before winding down to Arcadian villages that look as though they're preparing to tumble into the water.

History and nature merge here and stories abound of daredevil escapades and modern-day ingenuity. Staithes, with its sheltered harbour, rock pools, walkways and colourful houses that stoically face the wrath of the North Sea, has evolved from a fishing village into a thriving artistic community. The ruins of Whitby Abbey helped shape the Gothic work of Bram Stoker, and Scarborough, England's first seaside resort town, exudes contemporary holiday charm - amusements and ice-creams mixing perfectly with its sweeping beaches and castle, the latter found on the site of a Roman signal station and last attacked during the First World War. The locals of Robin Hood's Bay, once creative smugglers, now invite you to stop in for tea and admire their photogenic village nestled in the cliffs, while Saltburn-by-the-Sea proudly claims England's oldest functioning water-balanced cliff tramway and Yorkshire's last pier.

So choose a route and start your engines, as whatever the Yorkshire destination there's bound to be adventure and plenty of car-slowing, camera-grabbing scenery along the way.

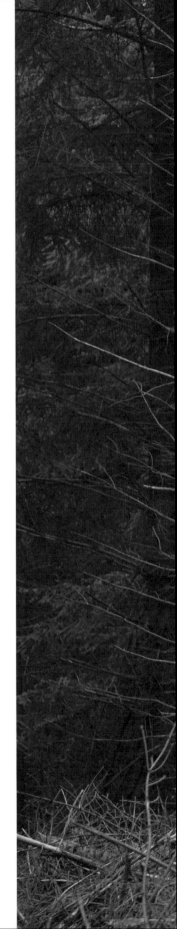

PIGGING OUT

Words by Angela Terrell & Annie Richards
Photographs by Georgina Skinner

The most English of hideaways.

I didn't know they snored, but grunts from slumbering pet pigs Darcy and Truffle provided fodder for thought as I contemplated their neighbours' impending trip to market. Surrounded by gardens brimming with nature's bounty, grazing chickens and beehives, the scene was the perfect reminder that great food comes from the land… and that nurtured pigs produce mighty fine bacon.

Nestled in the Mendip Hills, The Pig near Bath sets the bar for kitchen gardens - expansive and lovely - and while restaurants with gardens may seem commonplace, The Pig is more of a 'garden attached to a kitchen producing food at its most delicious for a restaurant with rooms'. Indeed, this home-away-from-home hotel - one of many to make up the ever-growing Pig family - is full of surprises. A stack of firewood by its entrance hints at the warmth within, while soft music, muffled chatter and velvet couches

envelop you further. Overlaid with personality, this muted background is the perfect canvas for a whimsical collection of treasures borrowed from various styles and eras; designer Judy Hutson skilled at making the eccentric feel charmingly chic. The bar, covered in bumps and grooves, is an old carpenter's bench, the light overhead is 'renovated' by rust, coloured glassware of every hue catches the sun's rays and artist David Farrer's papier-mâché animal heads watch over all.

Dining here really is a movable feast. Afternoon treats like chocolate tiffin are taken in the lounge, cocktails are sipped at the bar and savouries are found in the library. Candle-lit dinner in the conservatory with its mismatched furniture and vintage china is delightfully intimate, and everything from zucchini soup to rhubarb granita and blood orange syrup is a testament to the freshness and purity of garden-grown ingredients.

After such a meal (prefaced with revitalising treatments in the Garden Shed Spa or tramps past centuries-thick hedgerows) retiring to one of the 29 rooms is remarkably easy, the sumptuous bedding, country-style furnishings and claw-footed baths encouraging languishing dreams of future meals under the Mendip Hills' billowing clouds.

The Pig in Brockenhurst, found in a Georgian country house amidst rolling parkland, shares this appreciation for tranquil luxury and farm-fresh fodder. The hotel has the atmosphere of a gentleman's club, with discreet lighting, comfortable, squashy seating and roaring fires, all working to create an environment of generosity and indulgence where every need is catered to.

Stay in one of their rustic lodges and you'll find a well-equipped kitchen, complete with thoughtfully provided treats, cosy sitting room, wood burning stove and a spacious bathroom containing the most

wonderful monsoon shower - an evening meal the only thing capable of tearing you from such a setting.

As with their other hotels, the menu here is centred around the abundance of produce grown and reared in the grounds, with many additional ingredients sourced from within a 25 mile radius. My meal began with home smoked organic salmon and pancetta herb salad - pretty, crisp and delicious - followed by Brixham cod with a flower-strewn walled garden salad; the dish a perfect marriage of contrasting textures and flavours, elevated by the room itself, which emulates a fantasy greenhouse dotted with terracotta pots of fragrant herbs.

Reluctantly departing the following morning I felt relaxed and refreshed, nurtured by the enthusiasm and kindness of every member of staff. These hotels - unique yet united by their ethos - are convivial and luxurious, and ensure the best is made of everything, whether it's a broken garden pot or cocooning velvet couch.

thepighotel.com

TO THE
MANOR BORN

Words & Photographs by Liz Schaffer

Inspired by his home county, Michael Caines MBE has created a hotel where
food, design and the scenery reign supreme.

———————

We're on the sun-warmed stone terrace of Lympstone Manor, a farmhouse-turned-private-home-turned-luxury-hotel overlooking the pastel-hued Exe Estuary, 28 acres of landscaped gardens and a newly planted vineyard. There is salt in the air and rosé in our glasses, the setting blissfully serene.

Lympstone Manor is the creation of chef Michael Caines who, after nearly two decades at Gidleigh Park, longed for a project that was entirely his own - a space where he could express himself in more than just the kitchen. So he embarked upon a lengthy search for the ideal property, seeing the beauty within a crumbling Lympstone Manor the moment he found it. "When I came here," says Caines, "it was instantly obvious that the potential was massive. It had never been a hotel before, it was pretty run down, but the view, the sense of place ... I could just envision being here. This was what I was waiting for."

Caines' renovation combines contemporary and historic elements while taking full advantage of the Georgian structure's high ceilings and classical proportions. Meraki Design worked with Caines on the decor and each room - all subtly different - is inspired by a bird of the estuary, a theme that runs throughout the hotel, most noticeably in the wallpaper and watercolours of local artist Rachel Toll. Everything feels considered; opulent, playful and refined. There are beds to disappear into, roll top baths, splashes of marble, natural tones and Devon-infused *objects d'art*. "You can't escape the fact that we're in [such close] proximity to this wonderful estuary, so you've got to fit in and bring some of those external elements into the internal."

The world through the windows does indeed possess a siren call; you're summoned to cycle amidst the fields, stroll along Exmouth's shoreline and venture into the wilds of Dartmoor. But there's no rush. For now, you can simply sit in this oasis of calm, watching as the view evolves, the tidal estuary trying on different shapes and shades, slow moving and mesmeric. My friend, gazing at the clouds, paddocks and water from our balcony, recalls childhood summers by Devon's waterways - this is, after all, the realm of *The Famous Five*, and while the landscape may have a softness to it, there is still a wild sense of possibility, the hint of adventure.

Stunning as the setting may be, it's the Signature Tasting Menu that has tempted us here, an eight course culinary odyssey that showcases Caines' skill and Devon's offerings, paired with wines from a cellar of 600 bins; a meal designed to sate even the most discerning gourmands. "Devon is the third largest county in the UK, it's also one of the most prolific in terms of food production, in terms of quality of ingredients, in terms of farming and fishing," notes Caines. "We have amazing produce that is right within our landscape, from beef to pork to lamb to chicken, game, seafood, shellfish, it's all here. We have this incredible larder, early springs, late summers, beautiful landscapes which define Devon as a beautiful county but also as a food county."

"Devon is my home county, Exeter is my home town. This is where I grew up ... even if I searched the entire UK, I'd probably not have found anything as idyllic or beautiful, so it really does feel like a match made in heaven. I get a sense [Lympstone Manor] was just waiting for me to find it."

lympstonemanor.co.uk

Rydal Water, Cumbria

CHARLIE WAITE

Interview by Graeme Green

Getting a little lost remains an essential part of Charlie Waite's artistic practice; the simple act of wandering and exploring leading to a cornucopia of visual discoveries, all begging to be documented, frozen in time, transformed into something ethereal.

Beginning his creative career as an actor, Waite still loves losing his way after 40 years behind the lens, whether it's in the weather-worn English countryside, the rolling hills of Tuscany or Namibia's striking red deserts. This habit has served him well. Widely recognised as one of the world's great landscape photographers, Waite has been awarded a Direct Fellowship by the Royal Photographic Society and a prestigious Honorary Fellowship with the British Institute of Professional Photographers. His images are sometimes melancholic and contemplative, at other times playful and witty, captured in vivid colour or arresting black and white. He is fascinated by the power of light and shade; his understanding of these elements resulting in photographs that seem almost painted, dreamlike, not quite of this world. Always though, he tries to inject a bit of "soul" into his works and to create art that reflects how he felt the moment a photograph was taken.

Based in Dorset, Waite - who has over 30 international solo exhibitions to his name - now devotes much of his time to inspiring and guiding other photographers, whether it's by giving talks, holding exhibitions or leading tours and workshops with Light & Land, the company he founded in 1993.

You've travelled the world taking photographs. Do you feel England stands out when it comes to photogenic landscapes?

It certainly does. There are parts of England that offer landscape photographers real gems that have perhaps never been discovered before. I once set off on a day's photography and decided to go without a map and to intentionally try not to look at signposts. My plan was to attempt to get lost in the hope that I would find something. And find [it] I did, in the form of a heavenly avenue of trees.

One can still get lost in England. The key to becoming successfully lost lies with a simple rule - never travel along the same road twice. There are always good lanes in England. If water holds appeal, then there are stunning rivers … that are so worth following - but for these one does need a map, such are their twists and turns.

Does England have a particular character and is that something you attempt to highlight in your work?

I think it does. Thankfully there are still vast tracts of the English landscape that have little evidence of building. There are woods, magical and secret woods that even dogs and their owners haven't yet discovered.

The English landscape is as photographically rich as it ever was but, as with all landscape photography, the pursuit is the thing. Discovery, surprise, evaluation and interpretation lies at the heart of photography.

What do you think is England's most photogenic area?

Yorkshire gives me an enormous amount of pleasure. You get a great sense of history in Yorkshire with the drystone walls and the tough Yorkshire people who have to withstand some pretty tough weather. I especially like the Yorkshire Dales, the hills and the shapes. A place like Swaledale is hard to beat.

I'd probably say Win Green Hill near Shaftesbury in Wiltshire [is my favourite spot though]. It's where I can find good form. It's near where I live. I like it partly because it's [as if] … a giant has just scooped out a great big piece of soil and created a massive amphitheatre … like the Colosseum. The only things missing are the seats.

The measure of why I like a place is not necessarily because it makes a great photograph but because I feel incredibly good and calm there. It's like looking at a candle flickering.

You were an actor for the first decade of your professional life. How did you make the transition to photography?

My wife was in a popular BBC series called *The Onedin Line*, a bit like the *Downton Abbey* of its day, and I got bored of watching the filming. I had a Beetle in the 1970s, so I'd wander off into the Devonshire countryside while she was filming and found myself half-heartedly responding to a tree or a shed or a cloud. When I looked at the photos, I realised I'd had a much more profound feeling in those places and that the image hadn't [captured] that experience. That was the first sign for me that you have to invest more of yourself into a photograph.

How would you describe your approach?

I see it as contemplative and, using the word daringly, spiritual. I do have feelings about further dimensions. I'm in a state of permanent wonder and relish. The only time I can express that is through the camera.

Light & Land has been running since 1993. How has photography changed during its existence?

Digital has offered wonderful opportunities for so many millions of people to explore the magical world of photography. Yet some statistics show that 95 percent of all photographs made are either deleted or confined within an external hard drive, never to be set free. Digital has brought with it a degree of recklessness.

Irrespective of film or digital, over the last 25 years photography's given a very large number of people enormous creative joy, and that's what I care about more than anything.

What advice do you have for aspiring photographers?

Patience is crucial. Haste and pressure really are barriers to creativity, so you need to take your time … [and] fine-tune your sense of observation. Photography is about the eye, not about the equipment. Most of all, you need to be original. Try not to be too formulaic, and try to keep visually and mentally agile as you look around and explore a landscape. Missing a photographic opportunity is painful.

lightandland.co.uk
charliewaite.com

Image:
Willoughby Hedge, Wiltshire

Chesil Beach, Dorest

Stonehenge, Wiltshire

Uffington, Oxfordshire

Buttermere, Cumbria

JEZ TAYLOR

Interview by Liz Schaffer

Photographs by Tom Bunning

I'd encountered Daylesford Organic Farm's market garden once before, whilst working on a story for our inaugural magazine. *"Roaming through the market garden, even in the 'hungry gap' (that deceptive period at the start of spring when many vegetables decide to be difficult), you quickly embrace the thrill of foraging; of plucking purple sprouting broccoli from the ground as Gloucester Old Spots provide an unexpectedly melodic soundtrack."* It's four years on and later in the season, the broccoli replaced by curiously-shaped squash, but the project remains just as fascinating. Established by Carole Bamford, Daylesford has been farming organically for over 40 years and is led entirely by the seasons, making it a celebration of the land, with its team dedicated to outstanding produce, flavour and sustainability.

I have returned to spend a morning with organic horticulturist Jez Taylor, who manages Daylesford's market garden. Exuberant and passionate, he grows over 300 varieties of fruit and vegetables, alongside a range of cut flowers, and makes cider in the time he has spare. As we potter around the grounds his attention is constantly called elsewhere; to the crops that need him - "can we have a quick look at this?" - and the weeds that taunt. He constructs salads in the field, plucks tomatoes from vines and waxes lyrical about the region. His task here is mammoth but I doubt there's anyone better suited.

What drew you to horticulture and helped you understand the land?

I grew up amongst ornamental horticulturalists. My parents had a hanging basket nursery in the Vale of Evesham … I ended up with a pony and really enjoyed riding around the villages and bridle ways [seeing all that was going on]. In the mid-80s, agricultural subsidies were encouraging farmers to move hedgerows and plough up old grazing, on land which, historically, was always used for grazing … It was a real changing of the landscape and I started questioning why this was happening.

Did your parents' nursery business shape the way you work?

It gave me a work ethic because from a very early age I was doing piecework tasks for money. Filling pots with compost, filling seed trays, a penny a tray, that kind of thing. One of my favourite jobs was harvesting moss off the hillsides to line the hanging baskets. I could take the dogs, roam the countryside, gather moss and make some money. So that piecework, when you learn to work like that from an early age, it sets a standard for producing and you become very aware of productivity over time spent.

Daylesford is dedicated to all things sustainable and organic. What helped inspire these values in you?

I did a lot of WWOOFing and experienced a lot of alternative lifestyles through WWOOFing, like intentional communities … And then when I was at Reading University there were groups, like George Monbiot's The Land Is Ours, that started to question [why] it was so expensive to own land and then produce off the land and live in the countryside, and how unfair that is.

When I left university I took over two walled gardens attached to country houses. They charged me a peppercorn fee for rent but gave me access to sheds and water and in the end I was reaping all the benefits … Obviously I was in to growing food. I wanted to see how many different crops I could grow and how efficiently, how much money I could make. The more money you make as a grower the more staff you can employ and your life becomes easier.

When we started to have kids I wanted to move away from the Reading area. I had [a] cider business which I had going since early 2000 up in this part of the world, but I would just come up on the weekends, make the cider with a friend of my dad's and take it back to Reading where I'd sell it. You can make 7,000 litres of cider before you have to pay duty every year, so as part of a rational peasant's income stream, making cider is brilliant because the labour involved with it doesn't conflict with growing produce because if you do it in October or November, you've stopped planting, you've stopped weeding.

I totally believe that cider is the most environmentally sound alcoholic beverage to drink in this part of the world … You have these trees, some of which, like the ones in the carpark here, were planted between the wars, and year after year they throw out this fruit without you having to do anything, absolutely bugger all … Now the magic of the apple tree is that it takes all its water and nutrition out of the ground, right deep down, it doesn't compete with the grass around it, and it transforms that and … creates these apples which are between six and eight percent sugar. You can't get that in the vegetable world … You crush the fruit and you ferment that juice and you get cider. Eventually you realise that just using cooking apples in carparks isn't always going to make the best cider, but even then you can play around with the methodology.

How did you find Daylesford?

I started here in 2008 but found out about [Daylesford] in 2006 with the Thames Organic Growers, which is a group of growers in the Thames Valley [that gets] together periodically to look around each other's farms, compare notes, co-operatively buy things. In 2006 I came and looked around here as part of a Thames Organic group visit … We'd bought a house up here near my parents and I had the cider business going, [was working with the Eden Project] and was doing a bit of fancy gardening on the side, [but] I hadn't committed to anything proper, post leaving my Reading-based walled garden thing.

I was making the fire one day with a local newspaper and noticed this job and thought 'oh, that's interesting, market garden manager at Daylesford'.

This whole enterprise is set up based on Lady Bamford's message - organic is a good thing and we need to be looking after this country. The culture of growing things, farming things organically, needs support. If it's not supported we'll lose so many things. We'll lose skills and the knowledge to look after the land in a more sustainable way.

[Carole Bamford] is such a brilliant role model and figurehead for the business because she … takes this message and she preaches it wherever she goes. [She's created] vast numbers of jobs and nurtured artisan skills. That's what I grew up wanting to do.

We have it brilliant here and we should be singing and dancing about it, saying this is a blueprint, a model, because we're growing amazing crops that everyone is excited about and we're creating livelihoods. And we create this functional beauty in all the work that we do.

daylesford.com

Words by Graeme Green

TERRY GIBBINS

terrygibbins.com

Every cloud has a silver lining and in the case of black cab driver and photographer Terry Gibbins, even getting burgled had an upside. When his house was broken into several years ago, Gibbins decided that his camera equipment should remain with him at all times. "Keeping my kit with me in the [cab] is good practice really," says Gibbins, "because you never know when you might need a camera in London."

Originally from Greenwich, Gibbins has been a London taxi driver for 25 years and a photographer even longer, capturing his images in the early morning or evening - but if the conditions prove right he'll break whenever, assuming he doesn't have a fare. "Sometimes the opportunities pop up and you race across London. I've got a particular favourite photo of Battersea Power Station in the mist, taken one morning. I'd waited years for mist. It rarely [gets] foggy in London. When it is, I've already got my list of places I want to photograph. I'm good to go."

Gibbins' photography focuses primarily on landscapes, cityscapes and architecture, though a few of his passengers have also become his subjects. "London's got great photographic potential. It depends how people interpret it. You have to work at it. But the longer you spend there, the more you see."

Recently Gibbins began experimenting with water abstracts - the river he grew up by offering endless possibilities. "The Thames generates so much stuff for me to photograph. I cross the river several times every day. I love to go over Lambeth Bridge, with Battersea Power Station on my left, the Houses of Parliament on the right."

His photos also capture moments in the lives of Londoners. "I see all sorts. There's an old shot of mine at Sloane Square of this old Chelsea pensioner sitting on a bench, arms outstretched, chatting to a woman. There's probably an age gap of 40 years but she was absolutely fascinated by him. You see moments like that all the time. It's one of the things I like about driving a cab, every day is different."

lightandland.co.uk

Words by Liz Schaffer

HATTIE FOX

thatflowershop.co.uk

Hattie Fox has been a florist for half her life, working in a Notting Hill flower shop while obtaining art degrees from Camberwell, Central Saint Martins and The Slade School of Fine Art. After graduating with a Masters of Painting, Fox starting accepting freelance work, taking on commissions in exotic, experimental locations like India and New York; a florist before florists were cool.

"I came back and felt like I'd grown because I had all these amazing experiences and British floristry just wasn't there. It hadn't evolved into what it is now. It wasn't free." Her father, a gardener, suggested she begin her own business. And so she did, without really thinking about it. "I started in my house, which got a bit annoying for [the nine people] I lived with, so I [moved to] a little studio on Boundary Street in Shoreditch. I think I was just in the right place at the right time. There were no other florists around here which is kind of why I came, I didn't want to step on anyone's toes. One day the phone started ringing and it's never stopped."

Fox's Boundary Street studio was truly petite - there wasn't even a tap inside - so when Ace Hotel offered her a shop in their London property, she jumped at the opportunity. Here her style continued to evolve, the idea of a consistent aesthetic or colour palette not nearly as appealing as a challenge. During summer, she stocks around 70 percent British flowers, wonky and tremendous, largely sourced from New Covent Garden Market. "British flowers are amazing and I like how long the seasons are, so you see flowers from when they first come into the season all the way through … they change so much. To be in the game long enough to understand and appreciate that is really nice."

"You know when you're doing the right thing in your life. You get up and you're like, 'even though this is hard, [it's] what I'm [meant] to be doing'. I think I knew that the first day I worked in a flower shop; this is what my life is supposed to be, this is my path. When I'm away from flowers, I just want to go back to work. I don't like being away from flowers for very long."

VALENTINE WARNER

Valentine Warner created the Moorland Spirit Co. with his oldest friend, Walter Riddell, because it was right in front of them. Although the original seed may have been sown over a dinner months earlier, it was when tramping across Northumberland heath, through swathes of juniper bushes, that the pair discovered that everything they needed for a distillery already existed - moorland cloaked in trees, plants and herbs they'd be able to create endless drinks from.

They cut their teeth with cold climate gin, that most English of tipples, taking the spirit back to its roots, before moving on to more peculiar creations - concoctions distilled from pine needles and hawthorn. They played around, got experimental, picking juniper before it was ripe to give the gin youth and vibrancy, looking to the practices of the French perfume industry and allowing the natural environment to be their guide. "We're one of the few distilleries where you [go out] your front door and you're walking straight through a thicket of your botanicals," says Warner. "If you're standing under a Douglas fir tree and you can see junipers from the Douglas fir and from the junipers you can see the blackcurrants growing in the garden, then there's an environment there … When you stand in your land, among the very plants that grow there, a dictation takes place from this wild [space]."

An aficionado of food and the great outdoors, Warner is a cook with character who made a name for himself through his books, television programmes and food writing. He grew up in the hills of Dorset, which in the 70s remained incredibly rural, with parents who adored cooking and were wise to the world around them; but it was Warner's father who was the true nature enthusiast. "There wasn't a flower he didn't know the name of and when you went outside he expounded about the chattering spirits of the hedgerows … Everything outside I came to understand in terms of edible and inedible." Such an upbringing had a profound effect on Warner. Indeed, many of the ingredients he adores - wild sorrel, fish fresh from the river, mushrooms gathered on country ambles - are not those commonly found in stores; rather, they're the things that make cooking exciting. Given his taste for the largely unfamiliar, Warner labels his style 'international grandmother'.

"I cook with common sense. I cook from a deep love of ingredients. I don't cook things because they're convenient. If you hand somebody an artichoke you might as well have handed them a baby armadillo, they look horrified, [but] these things are so easy to cook. What I love to do is tell stories and I love to explain things to people. And I like to stand in a place, look around, understand an idea of its history, see what the market is like, see what is growing next to me and then make a decision, and I think that's what I'm all about."

At the heart of Warner's work is a belief in the value of grasping one's land and all that it affords. "There's a social environment of food around you which offers more than enough," he explains. "We have so much good stuff to eat that grows under our nose, in the wild. It's a place of wonderment, it's magical … [nature is our default setting, there's] nothing like walking into the sea for me to know where I belong."

Words by Liz Schaffer
Photographs by Tom Bunning

moorlandspirit.co

STANLEY DONWOOD

I've known Stanley Donwood - he of several names, assorted approaches, multifarious media, the chap who does the Radiohead artwork - for getting on ten years. I first met him at the simultaneous launch and closure of his record label, Six Inch Records, in a swish London bar - the sort of *boîte* where, when the bill arrives, people either pay without looking or start to cry. Donwood had bought a round of drinks and was looking sad having just gone bankrupt. Taking advantage of his frangible state, I introduced myself and asked if we could have a chat.

At the time I was writing a book about artistic space and process and for this I spoke to Donwood on several occasions in a succession of cold workshops and studios full of canvases, paint, linoleum and ink works in progress. In fact, during the time I've known him, looking back on the range and breadth of the work that he's created in the past decade, it's fair to say that cold studios are one of the few consistent elements of his practice.

The hypnotic linocuts of his new book, *Bad Island*, are just the latest in series of obsessively chiseled creations; the apocalyptic Vorticist vision of Los Angeles being pummelled by flash floods and meteors for the Atoms For Peace album *AMOK*, sequel to the black waters and tendril fires engulfing London on Thom Yorke's *Eraser* LP... and then there are the paintings - vibrant, fluid, branching capillaries of Radiohead's *King of Limbs*. Forests and spirits, fogs and benevolent monsters in oils; organic, mysterious, magnetic.

In 2012 we collaborated with writer Robert Macfarlane to make a slim volume named *Holloway*, a book that explores ancient landscapes and friendship - deep lanes, ghosts and bees; the story of three men hiding in a Dorset hedge, for which Stanley drew a set of beautiful pen and ink tree tunnels haunted by wraiths and spectres.

The cover and glorious silken innards of Radiohead's most recent album, *A Moon Shaped Pool*, features metallic liquid marblings, collage and cloud-form abstractions - waxy, viscous and erratic - harking back to the nebulous explosions of *In Rainbows* but new, unique and vital. Another tangent, another approach.

And in the midst of all this he's art-directed a film about atom bombs, written a couple of books and created covers for numerous records, and drawn a magic mountain vista for the cover of my book, *Climbing Days*. I felt giddy when I first saw it, the cross-hatched beast of the Dent Blanche front and centre, razor-backed and imperious. An astonishing picture. "Two pens." Donwood told me with his usual daft self-effacement. "Two pens and a few sheets of paper."

He once said that he has a horror of repeating himself. The next thing is always the most exciting thing; the chance to begin again, afresh. He thinks of himself as a commercial artist, a conduit for Radiohead's music, versatile and questing - always reacting and responding. The dream is to create artwork so different and diffuse that the audience thinks it's by a different person each time.

His dream is anonymity but in reality he's a remarkable Renaissance man with an international following. You can't win them all...

By Dan Richards   slowlydownward.com

THE LYGON ARMS

It's late spring in the Cotswolds, a tranquil pocket of England where honey-hued stone hamlets flourish between forests, meadows and waterways. Everything here appears golden, earthy, and at its quaintest when sun-kissed.

I'm in Broadway which, like many Cotswold villages, was a thriving settlement by the 12th century. It sits upon the 164 kilometre long Cotswold Way and is watched over by Broadway Tower, a Capability Brown folly that allows those who visit it to gaze across 16 counties. An old friend is visiting from Australia and I've brought her here to experience the most handsome, postcard-brought-to-life version of England possible.

This involves spending a night at the The Lygon Arms, a dog-friendly boutique hotel with a spa, design-centric rooms, Victorian-style indoor pool and history. Once a Tudor coaching inn, it has been at the centre of landmark political power plays and remains all dark wood and drama; the creaks of the uneven stone floors connecting the rabbit-warren of bars and seating areas, paired with rich wooden beams and antique furnishings,

adding character and warmth. The hotel's interior design is best exemplified by the Lygon Bar & Grill, once the coaching inn's great hall. The immense fireplace and vaulted ceiling are elegant nods to the past, while marble tables, plush leather chairs and antler-bedecked light features capture the hotel's more contemporary spirit.

Rather than being weighed down by the intrigue of bygone days, The Lygon Arms feels welcoming - a place of comfort, stories and quirk. Checking in, we're shown a small door near the entrance, once a passage for ladies of the night that led to a room frequented by Charles I. It was here that his supporters gathered during the English Civil War. Nearby is the Cromwell Room, now used for events and private dining, where Oliver Cromwell bunkered down for a presumably sleepless night on the eve of the Battle of Worcester. But as my friend and I settled in to this most English of abodes, pre-combat angst and political rivalry couldn't have been further from our minds. Instead we were considering rambles through rose gardens, morning massages and the Cotswold charms that lay in wait.

L. Schaffer

lygonarmshotel.co.uk

© S. Karppinen

CLIVEDEN HOUSE

Found five miles from Windsor Castle and long-adored by Europe's elite, Cliveden House is a place of temptation and style that has changed little since the 17th century, acting as a private house, university, hospital and - most recently - sumptuous, sophisticated hotel. More stately home than hideaway, Cliveden feels alive, playful almost; for while the interiors may be atmospheric - full of austere portraits, cascading chandeliers and the odd suit of armour - there is an openness to it all. The space is striking, inviting, keen to tell the tales of those who have walked its halls.

Looking out from my suite's window one glorious May morning - the opulent room decorated to feel particularly feminine and named after Sir Percy Blakeney, the Scarlet Pimpernel - I became lost in the romance of the Grade I listed formal gardens, the parterre melting into woodland that tumbled to the Thames. Owned by the National Trust and covering 376 acres, the grounds include a maze, pavilion, temple, amphitheatre and water garden complete with rhododendrons, herons, pagoda and koi.

Equally enticing is André Garrett's restaurant, where I indulged in an eight course tasting menu that showcased British seasonality and ingredients, the flower-adorned dishes akin to art - truffle risotto melts like butter while the seafood is unfathomably fresh. The paired wines were all natural, selected in part to surprise guests. A reminder that indulgence should always be vivacious.

You may also come here for afternoon tea, a jaunt in the Cliveden Spa or scandal alone, for Cliveden has long been the domain of theatrics and daring. It was here that Christine Keeler and John Profumo first crossed paths, from which the Profumo Affair went on to cripple the British Government. But the house was compelling from the start, purchased by the Duke of Buckinghamshire, a friend of Charles II, for his mistress Anna Maria. It has also been home to Elizabeth Villiers (William of Orange's lover), Princess Augusta of Saxe-Gotha and Nancy Astor, England's first female MP, who regularly hosted the likes of Charlie Chaplin and George-Bernard Shaw. Clearly Cliveden's flair for decadence and fine dining is long-standing.

L. Schaffer   clivedenhouse.co.uk

CHEVAL THREE QUAYS

Built on the site of a medieval wharf, you may not notice the subtle nods to history that fill London's Cheval Three Quays; the mosaics, stained glass and black and white photographs that honour lives and activities past. These details may be missed because the serviced apartments - which take their name from the long-gone Gallery, Chester and Brewer Quays - focus primarily on the luxurious. Everything here seems streamlined, soothing and homely. The beds of Tower View Penthouse are large enough to fill an entire room, their cosiness enhanced by muted tones and textured wallpaper. From the baths, mosaic glass vines climb the walls, and in the sitting room you're immediately drawn to the sculptural lighting feature, an assortment of pastel-hued glass globes that fall from above.

A feast could be prepared in the open, modern kitchen, and Champagne sipped on the terrace as the sun sets behind Tower Bridge, but the city beckons. Indeed, the most wonderful thing about Cheval Three Quays is its location. Overlooking the Tower of London, it is just across the water from the culinary delights of Borough Market and Bermondsey's restaurants, galleries and street stalls - antiques on Fridays, food all weekend. What more could one desire?

I. Hopewell   chevalresidences.com/cheval-three-quays

No.15 GREAT PULTENEY

I have always adored Bath, a city defined by Georgian stone and Roman wonder. It houses Magalleria and Mr B's Emporium - purveyors of fine magazines and books respectively - and is the site of many an Austen pilgrimage, although the author and Bath had a famously complicated relationship. I also love the city for No.15 Great Pulteney, a hotel near the Holburne Museum that is snug, avant-garde and art-besotted - a doll house brought to life.

By its entrance are portraits of Lobby Boys in Wes Anderson hues, hanging beneath kaleidoscopic chandeliers constructed from a vibrant assortment of glittering jewels. Antique pharmacy cabinets line the restaurant's walls and the bar's cocktail menu appears upon a set of playing cards.

Each room has its own creative nuances - be it floral sculptures growing from bathtubs or a stencilled canopy above the bed - while the spa's treatment rooms are part gallery. One is filled with hand-knitted socks, another brims with unconventional ceramics, while a third has what appears to be a reef-covered ceiling, the sculptures constructed from the rubbish responsible for coral's destruction. Comfort, curiosities and a social conscience, here excessive admiration is more than justified.

L. Schaffer   no15greatpulteney.co.uk

BOB BOB RICARD

Celebrated Soho restaurant, Bob Bob Ricard, serves a luxury English/Russian menu in the aurous glamour of its sumptuous all-booth dining room. Charming waiters hover in pink blazers, coachmen at an enchanted fizz party - the famous table buttons marked 'Press for Champagne' are enticing gilt trips in more ways than one. Effervescent high-camp sparkles throughout the restaurant - the menus, the service, the bar.

Our caviar starters dissolve on the tongue. Jersey rock oysters slip down smooth and salty, generous comfort eating for grown-up Bugsy Malones. Art Deco with ornate details and gold flourishes, Eastern influences in the foiled wallpaper, and flower arrangements to die for; drink enough bubbly and you might believe you were ensconced atop the Chrysler Building... in 1925. Luckily our mains arrive to ground us; a Chateaubriand which made me profoundly happy and a deliciously punchy salmon tartare. Across the aisle a couple are polishing off a beef Wellington, whispering superlatives between mouthfuls. The signature dessert provides a gloriously theatrical end to the night - a chilled chocolate bombe, a dark globe over which further chocolate (hot) is ceremonially poured to reveal mousse chocolate innards (marvellous). Delighted and disarmed, we set about our pudding with gusto, throwing moderation into Moskva, promising ourselves a return visit ASAP — BRB BBR!

© A. Gil   D. Richards   bobbobricard.com

ODDFELLOWS ON THE PARK

Framed by forest and hydrangeas, the historic Oddfellows on the Park, part of the curious and delightful Design Hotels collection, is like a classically tailored suit with an elaborate lining; the sensitively restored stone exterior provides no hint of the hotel's vivid and imaginative inner life.

Offering delectable food and delicately flavoured cocktails, the building in its current guise is as adaptable to guests' needs and desires as it has been to those of the surrounding community throughout its 150 year history. Weary travellers journeying to and from nearby Manchester Airport can eat well and repose, admiring the dreamy furnishings that fill the hotel's 22 rooms, whilst inquisitive historians can set about exploring the preserved 19th century Victorian details and Oddfellows' 100 acres of parkland, visible from every bedroom.

Those with time to spare may choose to spend a few days visiting nearby National Trust properties, like Quarry Bank and the Hare Hill gardens. Yet if scholarly endeavour and local touring are not enough, why not spoil yourself, indulging in a spa treatment at Pigsty, before absconding to the garden terrace, book in hand, for Champagne and contemplation.

T. Harrison   designhotels.com/hotels/united-kingdom/
                     manchester/oddfellows-on-the-park

TENTSILE

There is something particularly romantic about sleeping under the English stars, for this is a country made for camping; a place where it's remarkably easy to swap cosmopolitan madness for space, simple pleasures and silence. But the experience becomes all the more splendid when your feet no longer touch the ground. This is possible with Tentsile, a London-based company created by Alex Shirley-Smith that offers a range of unique tensioned tents you can suspend from trees - nature-friendly treehouse architecture at its most playful.

With a global following (and an outreach programme to match) Tentsile's story started in the early 80s when a six year old Shirley-Smith was moved by the plight of the Amazon Rainforest and, having recently discovered *Return of the Jedi*'s elevated Ewok village, suspected life among the trees was the environmental way forward - and so the journey began.

The Stingray is their flagship design, crafted to be portable, refined and wilderness-ready, and it's what comes with me into the English wilds. Because why shouldn't we embrace our inner child, sleep high above the forest floor and feel the joy of an alternative treehouse anew?

I. Hopewell   tentsile.co.uk

© A. Gil

WRIGHT BROS.

The Wright Brothers are Ben and Robin, brothers-in-law who began in bivalve wholesale before opening their first oyster bar in Borough Market. Their stated intention is to serve the best seafood in London, which is a tough ask - 'the freshest, the most accessible and the most fun' - but the Borough branch, one of five strung across the capital, is my local and I can attest to its wonders.

A long room with a bar running down the length and open kitchen at the back - antique signage, brass fittings, blackboards that read like bucket lists - a secret, hospitable space in which one can sit with a stout or wine and watch chefs shucking shells, searing sea bream, preparing their famous beef, Guinness and oyster pie or roasting Dorset crabs. The smells are tantalising. The golden fish pie is an institution and a drop of green Tabasco sets it off a treat. But it's the oysters I go for, each with their own character, shape and taste: Lindisfarne from Northumberland - delicate sea breeze; Jersey Rocks from the Channel Islands - silken sweet and steely; Caledonians from Loch Creran in Scotland pack a samphire tang; and the beautifully briny, firm and nutty Spéciales de Claire from Île d'Oléron, France. Heaven.

D. Richards   thewrightbrothers.co.uk

© A. Gil

HARTWELL HOUSE

Set in bucolic grounds under a Gainsborough sky, Hartwell House has an illustrious past that stretches back through years of English history. Part of the Relais & Châteaux and Pride of Britain Hotels collections, this partly Jacobean, partly Georgian house was once the seat of the noble Lee family, hosted King Louis XVIII of France and his exiled court, served as a Second World War army billet and emerged as a finishing school, before being lovingly restored by Historic House Hotels (the intricately carved staircase featuring Winston Churchill is a particular highlight) and opening to guests in 1989.

Those hoping for a classic country house experience will not be disappointed; Hartwell House provides a service straight out of the most luxurious English costume dramas. The lack of kettles in the 30 sumptuously appointed rooms is deliberate - instead, guests ring down for a tea tray that is brought directly to the room, complete with freshly baked biscuits.

If you're looking to counterbalance the hotel's cream teas, pre-dinner cocktails or deliciously traditional British menu (or simply enjoy some pampering), spend an afternoon in the hotel's spa and swimming pool. The best bit for city-dwellers seeking escape? It's less than an hour from London.

S. Kelleher   hartwell-house.com

© L. Schaffer

NEVER MISS AN ISSUE

Subscribe to *Lodestars Anthology* and have a little bit of wanderlust delivered right to your door.

A three issue subscription starts at £42.

Visit us online at

lodestars-anthology-magazine.myshopify.com

Here you'll also find a selection of back issues, bundles and copies of our book, *Pathways*.

The magazine's next destinations are Portugal and Switzerland.

© Renae Smith

DIRECTORY

Balmer Lawn
balmerlawnhotel.com

Battlesteads Hotel & Restaurant
battlesteads.com

Bob Bob Ricard
bobbobricard.com

Channel Adventure
channeladventure.co.uk

Cheval Three Quays
chevalresidences.com/cheval-three-quays

Chewton Glen
chewtonglen.com

Cliveden House
clivedenhouse.co.uk

Crabtree & Crabtree
crabtreeandcrabtree.com

Cyclexperience
cyclex.co.uk

Dark Sky Discovery
darkskydiscovery.org.uk

Daylesford Organic Farm
daylesford.com

Design Hotels
designhotels.com

Hadrian's Cycleway
hadrian-guide.co.uk

Haven Hall
havenhall.uk

Hell Bay Hotel
hellbay.co.uk

Historic House Hotels
historichousehotels.com

Imbarc
imbarc.co.uk

Le Blaireau
leblaireau.co.uk

Light & Land
lightandland.co.uk

Lime Wood Hotel
limewoodhotel.co.uk

Luxury Lodges
luxurylodges.com

Lygon Arms
lygonarmshotel.co.uk

Lympstone Manor
lympstonemanor.co.uk

National Stone Centre
nationalstonecentre.org.uk

National Trust
nationaltrust.org.uk

No. 15 Great Pulteney
no15greatpulteney.co.uk

Petersham Nurseries
petershamnurseries.com

Pride of Britain Hotels
prideofbritainhotels.com

Relais & Château
relaischateaux.com

Rick Stein, Sandbanks
rickstein.com/eat-with-us/rick-stein-sandbanks

Smedmore House
smedmorehouse.com

Tentsile
tentsile.co.uk

Thames Path
nationaltrail.co.uk/thames-path

The Cycle Hub
thecyclehub.org

The Landmark Trust
landmarktrust.org.uk

The Montagu Arms
prideofbritainhotels.com/hotels/the-montagu-arms

The New Forest
thenewforest.co.uk

The New Inn
tresco.co.uk/staying-on-tresco/the-new-inn

The Pig Hotels
thepighotel.com

Tresco Abbey Garden
tresco.co.uk/enjoying/abbey-garden

Vindolanda
vindolanda.com

Visit Isles of Scilly
visitislesofscilly.com

Visit Isle of Wight
visitisleofwight.co.uk

West Withy Farm Cottages
exmoor-cottages.com

Wright Brothers
thewrightbrothers.co.uk